Books by Yvonne Young Tarr

The Ten-Minute Gourmet Cookbook
The Ten-Minute Diet Cookbook
Love Portions
101 Desserts to Make You Famous
The New York Times Bread and Soup Cookbook
The Complete Outdoor Cookbook
The New York Times Farmhouse Cookbook
The Super-Easy Step-by-Step Wine Making Book
The Super-Easy Step-by-Step Sausage Making Book
The Super-Easy Step-by-Step Cheese Making Book
The Super-Easy Step-by-Step Book of Special Breads
The Up With Wholesome, Down With Store-Bought Book of
    Formulas and Recipes
The Tomato Book
The New Ten-Minute Gourmet Cookbook

THE NEW
Ten  *Minute*
GOURMET
COOKBOOK

Yvonne Young Tarr

Citadel Press ◀ *Secaucus, N.J.*

First paperbound printing, 1981

Copyright © 1976 by Yvonne Young Tarr
All rights reserved

Published by Citadel Press
A division of Lyle Stuart Inc.
120 Enterprise Ave., Secaucus, N.J. 07094

In Canada: Musson Book Company
A division of General Publishing Co. Limited
Don Mills, Ontario

Manufactured in the United States of America

ISBN 0-8065-0773-X

LIBRARY OF CONGRESS CATALOGING IN PUBLICATION

Tarr, Yvonne Young.
    The new ten minute gourmet cookbook.

    Includes index.
    1. Cookery. I. Title.
TX715.T2 1976   641.5   76-14806

. . . To my sons Jon and Nick who learned about gourmet cooking the hard way.

Contents

Foreword

A new way to gourmet!

 Stop!
Just this once read the foreword to your cookbook. It is important to you if you intend to get the most out of it: for herein lies a new way to gourmet.

For far too many years gourmet cooking has been spoken of in reverent whispers. For far too long many gourmet cooks have frightened away the competition by discussing food with more "inside phrases" than are used on Madison Avenue at high noon. It's *Sauce Béchamel* this and *Montmorency* that when all that needed to be said was "cream sauce" and "with cherries."

Good recipes were usually guarded with enough secrecy and mistrust to put the Society of Black Magic to shame. And why?

Simply to hide the fact that cooking, even gourmet cooking, is easy. And it is!

Look at it this way. Nearly every day of their lives, busy Italian and French and German and Spanish mothers cook what we call gourmet dishes. Look though any gourmet cookbook. The dishes that are mentioned are most often what Father gets for supper in some foreign land. To you and me they are exotic and glamorous but, to the woman who is cooking them, they are just tonight's steak and French fries. And conversely, of course, the ordinary meals you cook seem rare and exotic to them. So you see, you are already a gourmet cook to someone —perhaps that housewife in Brazil who is having only Angu Mineiro* for dinner tonight. So don't, for heaven's sake, let the thought of gourmet cooking intimidate you.

When I first started to cook, I opened a cookbook and made a crab soufflé. It turned out perfectly. No one had ever told me I should be afraid to try a soufflé. At that time I hadn't any idea it was the dish of kings. It just sounded good. After I had soufflés in several good restaurants and had heard the "oohs" and "ahs" that accompanied them, I became so terrified that I didn't try one again for many years. And yet, from the first time I made one to the present day, I have never had a failure with a soufflé, simply because cooking is easy. If you can read you can cook— and this book proves it!

Here, for the first time as far as I know, is a collection of delicious gourmet recipes, none of which is really complex. They are nothing but beautiful, mouthwatering, unusual dishes which, although they take ten minutes or less to cook, are actually indistinguishable from their hard-to-prepare counterparts.

*Brazilian lamb stew.

You'll find that none of them is hard to understand. This book doesn't tackle soufflés or French pastries. It isn't necessary. There are enough marvelous gourmet dishes that are ridiculously easy to make, especially with the techniques available today. Granted that when most gourmet dishes were invented, hours of preparation were necessary. But that was before canning, frozen foods, and modern appliances. How foolish we would be if we refused to use a blender only because Henry VIII's favorite chef didn't have one.

We who use this book have no such prejudices. We are concerned only with preparing gourmet dishes in minimum time and with maximum results. Any shortcut we can take, providing it does not alter the quality of the dish we are cooking, is fine with us.

More important than the mere aspect of time, however, is the fact that these recipes really work—not just occasionally, but every time. And what's more, they work with a minimum of confusion if you use this book properly. And by properly, I mean if you will get in the habit of following the carefully worked out, step-by-step directions.

You'll note, for example, that each recipe begins with a complete list of the ingredients and implements necessary to prepare it. (Naturally, cooking time begins once these items have been assembled.) These ingredient and implement lists are here to make your job as easy as possible and to speed up the time it takes to do the actual cooking as well. Get into the habit of using these lists properly, and you'll discover what a boon they can be. No more searching for that missing spice while the onions get too brown; no more turning the kitchen upside-down looking for the can opener only to find it, fifteen minutes and one burned omelet later, propping open the kitchen window.

Get into the "assemble first" habit and your cooking will go faster and smoother, your food will be properly cooked, and you'll be a lot more relaxed and happy about it, too.

Incidentally, another helpful feature to be found here is the "two-plus" system employed for feeding more than two guests. For example, while most recipes in this book are geared for two, merely add half a recipe more for each additional guest you expect, and cook away.

One word of warning. As I've mentioned before, the object of cooking even in a short time is to obtain the most satisfactory results. Don't try to set any speed records in the beginning. Deliberately slow down when cooking a dish the first time. Later when you are more familiar with the recipes you will find yourself speeding along and many dishes will take even less than ten minutes to prepare. Until then be content with merely cooking superb creations—every time.

But even above and beyond cooking, this book is intended to direct you to a more rewarding way of fulfilling your role as a gracious hostess. What good if your food is great but your kitchen sees more of you than your guests? On the other hand, who will care to come again if you are a darling hostess but dinner is dreadful? The answer lies in a perfect combination of the two. Now you can create the dinner of your dreams from the correct wine to the most delicate garnish, every time; and still have time for your guests to enjoy you, your personality, your charm, your hospitality. After all, that's what they came for, that's what they are entitled to, and that's what you will be able to give them with the help of this book.

A teacupful of tips

If you have something more important to do right now, such as whipping up a tantalizing tidbit, by all means do it. If you haven't and you'd like a few thoughts, tips, and assorted good-sense suggestions gleaned from fourteen years of gourmet cooking, by all means read this.

I don't intend to ramble on and fill your brain with hundreds of bits of information, most of which you will forget in a moment or less. When it comes to cooking, the phrases "learn from experience," "trial and error," and "learn the hard way," are trite but true. It would take thousands of words to describe accurately how it looks when a sauce "coats a spoon," or how thick a sauce is when it has "thickened slightly." These, I'll admit, are vague terms at best, but when you are cooking and suddenly, right on cue, a spoon becomes "coated" just as it says in the recipe, you automatically join the inner circle of cooks who "know" about coated spoons.

You need a good cookbook

Without doubt, the most important single aid in good cooking is a good cookbook: one that you can rely upon. I have quite a few cookbooks, some of which are better than others. Some I know will produce recipes that work. Every time! Others, I have learned from experience, have recipes that will need doctoring as I go along. A sauce may have to be thickened a little more or a flame may have to be lowered to prevent a cheese dish from turning mealy.

This is generally no disaster for an old hand at cooking, but for a beginner it can cause anything from heartbreak to complete and utter panic, depending upon who is waiting hungrily at table.

The first cookbook I bought after I was married was a costly but famous compilation of a thousand recipes. "A thousand recipes? A bargain!" I thought. "How clever of me!" True, it was expensive—but in the long run, with all those recipes . . .

I hadn't been clever at all! Nothing could have been more disappointing than that cookbook. There were so many tantalizing recipes to try, and try them I did with great patience and precision, but somehow they all cooked up into near misses. Either my "taster" was not tasting properly or gourmet food was just not as exciting as I had heard. What was wrong? Could it be—as I was afraid it might be—I?

At this moment, for all the world as it happens in fairy tales or television commercials, enter my mother with a skimpy little, unimpressive-looking cookbook. Out of mere good manners I tried it and found to my delight that anything I fixed from that book was sheer ambrosia.

The secret is in the testing

I have tried many cookbooks from that time to this. Some always worked, some worked some of the time, and others never worked, without my stepping in to correct something along the way, but until I wrote a cookbook myself, I never realized why some recipes perform perfectly and others do not. Now that I know the secret, it seems so obvious I blush to think it never occurred to me before. The secret is in the testing. My reliable little cookbook that worked so hard and well for me had been written by one man who took pride in every recipe and tested each with loving care. It is that conscientious concentration on testing that makes the difference.

Beware the large, stilted cookbooks!

If you are a brand-new cook, beware the large, stilted cookbooks that are little more than detailed listings of all the gourmet dishes in the world. Just because a dish is 400 years old does not mean there is only one way to cook it. Common sense alone will tell that the more recipes a cookbook has, the less time is taken testing each one. These large compilations are fine for the expert, but for the beginner or the sometime gourmet cook, it is best to buy smaller cookbooks that have had more individual attention. For example, every recipe in this, *The Ten-Minute Gourmet Cookbook*, has been tested anywhere from four to twenty times with pencil firmly behind ear, pot firmly in hand, and burns on the fingers to prove it. Cookbooks that are made up of separate recipes contributed by individual cooks or books that consist of recipes served as specialties of famous restaurants are usually excellent also. These again contain special recipes that have actually been proven to be not only delectable but predictable too. Reputations ride on every recipe.

Courage! Don't be afraid of anything!

The second most important element in cooking is courage. Fortify yourself with a good cookbook, and forge ahead courageously. Don't be afraid of anything! Pick out a recipe, purchase the necessary ingredients, assemble the proper utensils, allow yourself plenty of time, concentrate, and cook away! Nothing can happen but delicious food. The world doesn't depend upon the outcome of your meal. No heads will roll if your entrée isn't precisely the way you want it. As a matter of fact, in most cases your guests probably do not dine nearly as well at home, so for your own sake, relax!

Be a guest at your own party

If I were queen of all the kitchens of the world, I would make it a law that every time guests were due for dinner, a recipe brand-new to the cook, would have to be tried. It has been my experience that cooks never wield their cooking fingers with better results than when tackling an exciting recipe for the first time. Ingredients get measured precisely. Sauces get stirred for the proper length of time. Results? A *perfectly* prepared whatever-it-is. There is no blurring of the beautifully balanced results because of carelessness inspired by overconfidence. Then, too, there is the added enjoyment of experiencing, at the same time your guests do, the tasty concoction you have so carefully prepared. It's just like being a guest at your own party.

How to avoid last minute-itis

Whenever you can prepare the initial stages of a recipe in advance, do so. If possible, whip up the chosen dish in its entirety and set it aside until needed. Naturally, this will not always be practical. I have marked with an asterisk the specific recipes that are easily prepared ahead of time, and have indicated just how far along they may be brought prior to serving without endangering their deliciousness. When it is necessary to do any last-minute cooking, always be sure the needed ingredients and equipment, serving dishes and spoons are neatly assembled and ready for instant action.

It takes a great deal of patience and planning to produce a dinner party that really comes off. The menu section of this book offers advice that applies to the aesthetic aspects of choosing a menu. Under this, the practical section of the book, may I suggest another consideration in menu making: how to avoid last-minute-itis. Never choose more than one recipe that calls for a great deal of last-minute attention. Gear your menu not only to good eating, but to the time you have available.

After years of experimenting, I have found an almost foolproof system of serving a dinner for eight either unassisted or with one inexperienced helper.

If you have several in help or are in the habit of hiring specially trained help when you entertain, the limitations imposed by your menu need not be so strict. You need concern yourself only with bringing the courses to be served up to the step prior to serving, instructing the persons employed—either orally or with detailed lists—and hoping no power struggles occur in the kitchen, at least not until after dessert.

However, if you are, as I am, often forced to serve either alone or with a neophyte helper, the following plan works wonderfully well.

THE DAY BEFORE THE DINNER PARTY

1. *Decide upon your menu, including the necessary wine or wines.*

   Select at least three hors d'oeuvres that can be prepared in their entirety either several hours or a day in advance of your party. Keep in refrigerator until needed.
   (Eliminate soup course for a minimum amount of trouble.)
   Pick a salad that can be ready to place on the table in individual plates when the hors d'oeuvre dishes are removed.
2. *Make a list of everything needed.*
3. *Do your shopping.*

THE DAY OF THE DINNER PARTY

1. *Midafternoon*
   Get the dining room ready for your guests.
   (a) Set the table for dinner no later than 2:00 in the afternoon.

(b) At the same time, set up a sideboard or extra table with the serving plates and silver that will be needed.

(c) Close doors to dining room.

Cook dinner for children (something that can be popped into an oven set at any temperature, warmed, and served with a minimum amount of trouble).

Prepare the following as far as possible in advance.

(a) Soup

(b) Entrée

(c) Salad

(d) Vegetables

(e) Dessert

Wash utensils used in above.

Assemble and stack on one counter all ingredients and utensils needed to complete recipes.

2. *Early evening*

Give children dinner, hungry or not.

Take bath and get dressed. During bath, make out instruction list for helper. (This is not easy if you are a shower-taker.)

Turn down children's beds, put out pajamas, give children any last-minute instructions.

3. *Just before guests arrive*

Complete whatever dishes will not be ruined by keeping warm until dinner.

Put ice in ice bucket and set out glasses on a tray.

Open wine.

4. *As the doorbell rings*

Wash hands.

Join husband and guests during predinner drinks.

5. *Just before dinner*
   Place hors d'oeuvres on table.
   If hot soup is to be served, place on low flame.
   Make salad.

6. *During dinner*
   While hors d'oeuvres are being consumed, have helper
      ladle soup into soup plates. Tell her to wait eight min-
      utes after everyone is seated.
   After hors d'oeuvres, assist helper in removing hors
      d'oeuvre dishes.
   Assist helper in serving soup.
   If not serving soup, serve salad after removing hors
      d'oeuvre dishes.
   Instruct helper to remove soup plates and serve salad.
   Meanwhile, complete entrée and place vegetables in serv-
      ing dishes.
   Assist helper in carrying entrée and vegetables to side-
      board.
   Instruct guests to serve themselves.
   Meanwhile, pour wine.
   Enjoy dinner with your guests.
   Have helper boil water for coffee and/or tea.
   When your guests have been satisfied, instruct helper to re-
      move all plates and food from table and sideboard.
   Meanwhile, set coffee and tea to brewing and complete
      dessert.
   If dessert is to be flamed before your admiring guests,
      carry dessert to table, flame it, and serve.
   Instruct helper to place cups and saucers beside your place
      at the table.
   Serve coffee.
   When dessert is finished, suggest a brandy in the living
      room.

Exit guests, host, and hostess from dining room, closing
   doors behind them to permit helper to work her magic
   with the dirty dishes.
FINIS   DINNER

Good grief! Here they come . . .

The most severe test in hostessing—or just plain homemaking,
for that matter—is not the prearranged, preshopped, "dinner
at eight" kind of entertaining but rather the "Good grief!
Here they come up the front walk at mealtime and I haven't a
thing in the house" kind of emergency cooking. A device I em-
ploy to render this monstrous situation completely harmless is
to have a checklist of ingredients tucked away in the kitchen
cupboard or the freezer ready to be transformed into ambrosia
at practically a moment's notice. Two things may be accom-
plished by using this list:

1. A variety of menus may be prepared *in their entirety,* relying
solely on the items here mentioned.
2. The remainder of recipes in this book may be prepared simply by purchasing several *main* ingredients, thus reducing shopping time and inconvenience to a bare minimum.

Naturally, it is not *necessary* to stock all the items mentioned
below, but the more of these gourmet aids that find a perma-
nent home in your kitchen, the more inclined you will be to
whip up something exotic when the occasion demands. Thus
your ascendance from a scrambled-egg cook to chef *formi-
dable* will be accelerated considerably merely by the purchase

(over a period of time, if necessary) of the listed items. Please, don't let the length of lists frighten you. The staple items you no doubt keep handy already, the spices take up very little room and last a long time, and the frozen foods, wines, cheeses, canned goods, hurry-ups, and gourmet staples, once purchased, may not need to be replaced for many, many months.

If you find you are missing many of the gourmet items in the following lists don't be discouraged. Merely add one or two of these interesting foods to your collection each week and soon your kitchen will be as intriguing as a magic shop and just as capable of producing magic.

STAPLE ITEMS

. . . Butter	. . . Pepper
. . . Flour	. . . Bacon
. . . Milk	. . . Cooking oil
. . . Sugar	. . . Mayonnaise
. . . Bread	. . . Spaghetti
. . . Eggs	. . . Minute rice
. . . Heavy cream	. . . Prepared mustard
. . . Onions	. . . Catsup
. . . Salt	. . . Honey

These staple items should be found in any well-stocked kitchen. Mark how many you have in yours and check your score below:

(18) . . . *Your kitchen's a pleasure* (10) . . . *Barely adequate*
(5) . . . *Your family is starving to death!*

SPICES AND HERBS

. . . Cinnamon	. . . Curry powder
. . . Cloves	. . . Fennel seed
. . . Parsley flakes	. . . Tarragon
. . . Garlic powder	. . . Chervil

. . . Paprika	. . . Basil
. . . Nutmeg	. . . Whole cloves
. . . Marjoram	. . . Stick cinnamon
. . . Thyme	. . . Whole pepper
. . . Dried mint leaves	. . . Dill
. . . Oregano	. . . Sage
. . . Dry mustard	

The spices on your shelf, like the lines in your palm, can tell more about you than you may suspect. Mark off the ones on *your* shelf and check your score below:

(21) . . . Why don't *you* write a cookbook? (12) . . . You're a whiz! (5) . . . You're off to a good start. Keep collecting!

GOURMET STAPLES

. . . Olive oil	. . . Shallots
. . . Croutons	. . . Wine vinegar
. . . Anchovies	. . . Garlic (whole)
. . . Anchovy paste	. . . Soy sauce
. . . Bread crumbs	. . . Worcestershire sauce
. . . Capers	. . . French dressing
. . . Chutney	

These items show up more frequently in gourmet cooking than do the bread-and-milk-type staples. How many do you consider indispensable?

(13) . . . Want to trade recipes? (8) . . . Invite me to dinner! (3) . . . You show promise—get out of that rut!

The following are hurry-up and substitute items not generally stocked. However, as these are frequently mentioned in this book it would be a good idea never to be without them.

HURRY-UPS

Frozen red and green pepper*
   (see page 235)
Frozen onion
   (see page 237)
Frozen mushrooms
   (see page 243)

Freezer rice
   (see page 242)
Frozen chives
   (see page 239)
Frozen tomato purée
   (see page 241)

* Uncooked, chopped frozen green pepper and onion are readily available in the stores where I shop. You may find items available to you that are even better. Never hesitate to try new shortcuts you may discover at your store. If on the other hand you cannot find the above groceries at your food store, I would suggest you prepare and freeze your own so as always to have them handy.

CANNED GOODS

Beef consommé
Cream of chicken soup
Minced clams

Tomato paste
Pimiento
Mushrooms

FROZEN FOODS

Shrimp (cooked and cleaned)
Thin sliced rare roast beef

Cooked lobster meat

In addition, these wines and cheeses, used most often in gourmet cooking, are ideal to round out the perfectly stocked kitchen.

CHEESE

Blue cheese
Mozzarella
Grated Swiss

Grated Cheddar
Grated Parmesan

WINES, LIQUORS, LIQUEURS

Red wine (for cooking)
White wine (for cooking)

Sherry
Cognac

In addition, a "neutral" red and a white wine and perhaps a rosé are nice to have on hand to dress up a spur-of-the-moment meal that must be planned when liquor stores are closed.

SPECIAL GOURMET ITEMS

If gourmet items such as truffles, pâté, etc., are not readily available in your area, do not despair. Most large department stores in bigger cities have gourmet departments and will be delighted to mail them to you.

Reminder!

Most recipes geared for two; simply double for four, or add half a recipe more for each additional guest.

All ingredients are presumed to be well washed and properly trimmed.

*Note starred recipes can be prepared in advance, either completely or partially. Refer to footnotes for specific recommendations.

Hors d'oeuvres

Golden promises

Your guests have assembled. There has been the usual greeting, chatting, laughing and perhaps drinking. You've been enjoying the party as much as your guests, but now it's time to serve dinner. You slip into the kitchen where you have prepared every recipe, as far as was possible, in advance. You finish the preparation of the first course and lead your guests to the table.

Now! Your guests have been invited for dinner. This is perhaps the one moment in an evening that centers around dinner when the food has the complete attention of its audience. Conversations have been broken off; chairs have been settled. Your audience is in the palm of your hand. Don't just stand there—enchant them!

Give them some luscious morsel that says, "See what you have in store?" Woo them with some tantalizing tidbit that cautions, "Don't blink an eye or you may miss something fantastic." Your guests are expectant. Lead them to expect even more. Let the hors d'oeuvre promise them the most delicious dinner they ever tasted, and then see to it that they're not disappointed.

MUSHROOMS STUFFED WITH WALNUTS AND PISTACHIOS, GLAZED

If you are looking for a first course that is daringly different, yet filled with flavor everyone will enjoy, sample this. Who could help but love hot and bubbling mushrooms, walnuts and pistachios with chutney? Don't hesitate to try it. It's really delicious.

INGREDIENTS
4 tablespoons butter
8 large mushrooms
½ cup chutney
¼ cup shelled pistachios
¼ cup chopped walnuts

ASSEMBLE
skillet
paring knife
measuring cup
spoon
flameproof baking dish

DIRECTIONS
Light broiler and set at high heat. Melt butter in skillet over medium flame. Peel mushrooms if necessary and chop stems. Add mushrooms to skillet and sauté for 4 minutes, turning once. Remove caps from pan. Measure chutney and add to skillet. Chop any large pieces of mango, etc. into half-inch dice. Add pistachios and walnuts. Stir-cook for one minute. Stuff mushroom caps with mixture in the skillet. Serve hot.

GARNISH *(Optional)*
Top each mushroom with small piece candied cherry and 2 green halves of pistachio nut, set like a flower with green leaves. Decorate plate with sprigs of watercress.

MOZZARELLA IN CARROZZA

This tasty little sautéed sandwich comes to the table all hot and golden and oozing with goodness in the form of mozzarella cheese. Is it any wonder it is adored by epicures half the world round?

INGREDIENTS
8 thin slices white bread
8 tablespoons butter
2 tablespoons olive oil
1 egg
1 tablespoon milk
4 ¼-inch slices mozzarella cheese
8 strips anchovy paste
¾ cup fine bread crumbs

ASSEMBLE
medium-sized skillet
set measuring spoons
cookie cutter or glass
fork or egg beater
shallow bowl (for egg)
plate (for bread crumbs)
sharp knife or cheese cutter

DIRECTIONS
Cut bread into rounds with cookie cutter. Heat 4 tablespoons butter and 2 tablespoons olive oil in skillet. Beat one egg and one tablespoon milk together in bowl. Butter one side of each slice of bread. Cut cheese slices into rounds with cookie cutter. Place one slice cheese on every other buttered slice bread, make an x of anchovy paste on each and top with another bread round (with butter in center of sandwich). Dip mozzarella sandwich in beaten egg, then dip in bread crumbs, and fry in oil until golden, turning once.

GARNISH *(Optional)*
Place a rolled anchovy fillet in the center of each serving and tuck a small piece of parsley on either side of this. Serve very hot.

RAMEKINS OF SHRIMP IN SOUR CREAM

Succulent shrimp and mushrooms in a rich, pink sour-cream sauce. For a tempting opener to a very special meal, you couldn't do better than this.

INGREDIENTS
5 tablespoons butter
1 6-ounce package cooked and
   cleaned frozen mushrooms
   or Your Own Freezer
   Mushrooms (see page 243)
8 large cooked and cleaned
   shrimp, available at your fish
   store
¾ cup sour cream
1 teaspoon Chinese soy sauce
2 teaspoons paprika
¼ teaspoon salt
4 tablespoons grated Swiss cheese
   or Cheddar cheese, available
   in packages

ASSEMBLE
medium-large skillet
measuring cup
tablespoon
set measuring spoons
small saucepan
2 large ramekins or individual
   fireproof casseroles

DIRECTIONS
Melt the butter in the skillet over medium heat, add the frozen mushrooms and the shrimp and cook for 3 minutes. Meanwhile, heat the sour cream, soy sauce, paprika and the salt in the small saucepan over low heat. Add the sour-cream mixture to the shrimp and cook, stirring constantly for 2 minutes. Divide into ramekins, sprinkle with grated cheese and place under broiler until cheese melts. Serve immediately.

COQUILLES ST. JACQUES*

A melt-in-your-mouth mixture of scallops, white wine, butter, and Parmesan cheese. A favorite French first course.

INGREDIENTS

3 shallots, peeled, or Your Own
   Freezer Shallots (see page 239)
4 large scallops (uncooked)
5 ounces Your Own Freezer
   Mushrooms (see page 243)
3 tablespoons butter
1 tablespoon white wine
2 tablespoons plus 2 teaspoons
   fine bread crumbs
1 tablespoon heavy cream
2 teaspoons grated Parmesan
   cheese

ASSEMBLE

food grinder
skillet
paring knife
set measuring spoons
2 large coquille shells for
   cooking and serving

DIRECTIONS

Turn broiler to high heat. Run the shallots, scallops, and half the mushrooms through food grinder using fine blade. Melt butter in skillet. Add the ground mixture, one tablespoon white wine and the remainder of mushrooms, chopped. Cook for 2 minutes over medium high heat, stirring constantly. Lower heat if mixture begins to stick to pan. Stir in heavy cream and 2 tablespoons of the bread crumbs. Turn off heat.*

To serve, heat coquilles slightly in pan, then heap onto coquille shells. Sprinkle each with one teaspoon bread crumbs and one teaspoon Parmesan cheese. Place under broiler flame until slightly browned. Serve hot.

* May be prepared to this point 24 hours in advance and refrigerated until serving time.

FRESH MUSHROOMS IN DOUBLE CREAM

Never tasted raw mushrooms? Serve this pale and delicate first course at the first possible opportunity. When uncooked, that perfection the mushroom has a flavor and texture subtle in the extreme. Serve with White Bean and Anchovy Salad. Eggs à la Russe, and Onion Salad as one of a selection of hors d'oeuvres.

INGREDIENTS
8 fresh, large mushrooms
1 cup sour cream
½ cup heavy cream
12 drops Tabasco sauce
paprika

ASSEMBLE
paring knife
medium-sized mixing bowl
measuring cup
spoon
bowl for serving

DIRECTIONS
Peel mushrooms if necessary, discard tough stems and cut caps into paper-thin slices. Mix sour cream, heavy cream, and Tabasco sauce. Add mushrooms to the cream mixture and mix gently, taking care not to break up slices. Place in serving bowl. Serve cold.

GARNISH
Sprinkle bowl with paprika. Decorate center of bowl with 4 mushroom slices.

ESCARGOTS IN CREAM

Snails dressed in a sauce that's different and delectable . . . a creamy new way to serve this gourmet's delight.

INGREDIENTS

2 tablespoons butter
1½ teaspoons flour
½ small onion or 2
    tablespoons Your Own Freezer
    Onions (see page 237)
1 7½-ounce can snails, drained
1 cup heavy cream
2 egg yolks
salt and white pepper to taste
4 toast points or prepared patty
    shells

ASSEMBLE

medium-sized skillet
set measuring spoons
sharp knife
can opener
strainer
measuring cup
small saucepan
stirring spoon
mixing bowl
fork or egg beater
2 small serving plates

DIRECTIONS

Melt butter in skillet and stir in flour. Chop onion and add to skillet. Drain snails in strainer and add to the butter-flour mixture with ½ cup of the cream. Stir well and simmer while you beat the 2 egg yolks in a mixing bowl. Beat the other ½ cup of cream into the egg yolks. Pour the egg-cream mixture into the skillet and cook over low fire, stirring constantly until thickened. Do not let mixture boil or egg yolks will curdle. Add salt and white pepper to taste. Serve immediately in hot patty shells or on toast points.

GARNISH *(Optional)*

Tuck tiny pieces of parsley around the edges of the serving dishes. Sprinkle with nutmeg. Serve hot.

FRESH VEGETABLES WITH TUNA DIP*

Crisp scallions, radishes, carrot sticks and juicy cherry tomatoes arranged around a "dip" with a difference. The secret ingredient? Tuna fish. Served at one of New York's favorite French restaurants as a between-course treat, this makes something wonderful to serve with drinks.

INGREDIENTS

2 large carrots, scraped
8 scallions, trimmed
10 radishes, with stems
16 cherry tomatoes, with stems
½ of a 3¼-ounce can tuna
2 tablespoons milk
2 tablespoons mayonnaise
1 small onion, peeled and chopped
½ cup sour cream
2 tablespoons heavy cream

ASSEMBLE

potato peeler
blender
paring knife
set measuring spoons
mixing bowl
serving plate
bowl for dip

DIRECTIONS

Cut carrots into strips ½ inch wide and 3 inches long. Cut roots from radishes. Plunge all vegetables into icy water and refrigerate until needed. Open tuna and drain. Put ½ can tuna, milk, mayonnaise, onion and sour cream into blender. Blend 1½ minutes. Add heavy cream. Mix. When ready to serve, place tuna dip in bowl. Drain vegetables and arrange attractively around the dip. Serve cold.

GARNISH *(Optional)*

Decorate top of dip with a design of flowers and leaves cut from carrots, radishes, and scallion greens.

N O T E
To serve 4, double quantity of vegetables only.

* May be prepared several hours in advance of serving. Refrigerate until needed.

GUACAMOLE
(serves 4 to 6)

There's no sense preparing a small quantity of this superb South-of-the-border hors d'oeuvre since it is such a party favorite. Any leftover portion may be thinned with heavy cream,* chilled, and served as a cold soup the next day. Versatile, isn't it?
Do not prepare more than one hour prior to serving, or avocado may darken.

INGREDIENTS
1 avocado
1 small onion
1 clove garlic, peeled
1 tomato
½ teaspoon chili powder
¼ teaspoon salt
1 teaspoon lemon juice
2 tablespoons mayonnaise
corn chips

ASSEMBLE
sharp knife
small mixing bowl
set measuring spoons
garlic press
spoon
2 small glass bowls

DIRECTIONS
Peel and seed avocado. Peel onion and crush garlic. Finely chop avocado, tomato and onion. Mix chopped vegetables, garlic, chili powder, salt, lemon juice and one tablespoon mayonnaise. Place in glass bowl and spread remaining tablespoon mayonnaise over the top of the dip. Serve with corn chips.

* To prepare Guacamole Soup, stir heavy cream into leftover dip immediately following serving, or avocado will darken. Refrigerate.

ITALIAN ANTIPASTO*

Here's a delightful way to begin an Italian meal, or almost any other. Even the most stubborn appetite won't be able to resist so many tempting tidbits.

INGREDIENTS

1 green pepper
1 tomato
4 scallions
4 leaves lettuce
1 3½-ounce can tuna fish
6 slices canned chilled beets
4 anchovy fillets
8 strips of pimiento
2 thin slices Provolone cheese
2 slices Italian salami
6 cold cooked shrimp, available
  at your fish store
8 black olives
8 green olives
¼ cup olive oil
2 or 3 tablespoons wine vinegar

ASSEMBLE

can opener
colander
paper towels
paring knife
large serving plate

DIRECTIONS

Wash green pepper, tomato, scallions, and lettuce and blot dry with paper towels. Arrange lettuce to cover serving platter. Drain beets and tuna. Place whole can of tuna in center of serving plate. Slice tomato. Discard stem and pulp from green pepper and slice pepper into one-inch strips. Arrange anchovy fillets, tomato slices, green pepper, scallions, pimiento, cheese, and salami attractively around the tuna. Garnish with shrimps, olives, and beet slices. Dribble ¼ cup oil and 3 tablespoons wine vinegar over everything but the fish. Serve cold.

* May be prepared one or two hours in advance. Follow recipe up to point where olive oil and wine vinegar are added. Refrigerate. Continue recipe several minutes before serving.

TARTAR SANDWICHES

Looking for something hearty to serve with drinks? These tasty uncooked steak sandwiches are sure to be a hit!

INGREDIENTS
1 sweet onion, finely chopped
8 thin anchovy fillets
4 small slices rye bread
½ pound ground lean steak. Ask your butcher to put it through the grinder that has not been used for pork.
1 egg yolk
44 capers
2 stuffed olives, sliced

ASSEMBLE
paring knife
small bowl or cup for egg yolk
fork
pastry brush
paper towels
serving plate

DIRECTIONS

Peel, wash, and chop onion. Blot anchovies on paper towels. Spread bread with chopped meat. Beat egg yolk with fork. Brush outer 1″ of meat with egg yolk. Press chopped onion into egg-brushed meat. Crisscross tartar sandwich with anchovy fillets. Decorate uncooked meat with 10 capers per sandwich. Put 1 slice olive where anchovy fillets cross. Place 1 caper in the center of each olive slice. Serve cold.

FRESH FIGS AND WALNUTS IN PROSCIUTTO HAM CONES*

Here's another opener that comes to us from Italy. Fresh figs rolled in walnuts and wrapped in thin slices of pink prosciutto ham. A beautiful start to any meal.

INGREDIENTS

10 sprigs watercress
4 fresh figs
4 large slices prosciutto ham
1 egg white
¼ cup finely chopped
   walnut meats

ASSEMBLE

paring knife
fork
small plate
small bowl
paper towels
pastry brush
2 small serving plates

DIRECTIONS

Wash the watercress and trim any tough stems. Wash figs. Dry both on paper towels. Arrange watercress on serving plates. Roll the prosciutto diagonally, with one end closed and one end open, to form a cornucopia or cone. Place egg white in small bowl. Beat with fork. Brush fig lightly with egg white. Roll in nut meats. Insert the ripe fig in prosciutto cone. Place in the bed of watercress. Serve cold.

NOTE

To serve 4, double all ingredients but egg white.

* May be prepared an hour or two in advance of serving.

It is always a good idea to serve toothsome "nibbles" along with drinks. The four that follow are particularly pleasing.

CRUNCHY CHINESE CHICKEN BALLS

INGREDIENTS
1 chicken breast, skinned, boned
  and ground (your butcher will
  generally do this for you if
  you ask nicely)
1½ tablespoons miso paste*
⅛ teaspoon salt
5 water chestnuts
1 teaspoon flour
3 tablespoons vegetable oil

ASSEMBLE
mixing bowl
mixing spoon
sharp knife
set measuring spoons
medium-sized skillet

DIRECTIONS
Mix the ground chicken in a bowl with the miso and salt. Mince the water chestnuts and add them, along with the flour, to the meat. Shape into balls about one inch in diameter and fry in hot oil for 3 to 4 minutes or until brown on all sides. Serve hot with Sweet and Mustard-y Dipping Sauce (see page 231).

*Available in health-food stores and Oriental groceries.

ITALIAN POLPETTE
(Meatballs)

The Italians have their own special way of seasoning a mixture of lemon peel, garlic and parsley. This mixture, called gremolada, *gives a zesty and distinctive flavor to these thoroughly gourmet meatballs.*

INGREDIENTS
zest or thin yellow layer
   of skin of ½ lemon
2 teaspoons Your Own Freezer
   Parsley (see page 240)
1 small clove garlic, peeled and
   crushed
6 ounces ground fairly lean beef
2 pinches vegetable salt flavoring
⅛ teaspoon ground nutmeg
1 slice bread
2 tablespoons milk
2 tablespoons beaten egg
3 tablespoons vegetable oil

ASSEMBLE
fine grater
small bowl
set measuring spoons
garlic press
2 cups
fork
medium-sized skillet

DIRECTIONS
Scrape uncut lemon gently against grater until the thin yellow lemon skin has been removed (do not include any of the bitter white underskin. Save the lemon for some future use). Add lemon zest, parsley, garlic, ground beef, vegetable salt and nutmeg to bowl. Crumble bread into one cup, add the milk, then squeeze the bread dry and add it to the ingredients in the bowl. Beat the egg in the second cup. Add 2 tablespoons beaten egg to bowl. Mix ingredients lightly with fingers or fork. Still handling gently, form beef mixture into balls less than one inch in diameter. Heat the oil in the skillet, add the meatballs, and cook over medium flame until brown on all sides. Serve hot.

NEAPOLITAN MEATBALLS

Neapolitan but not typically Italian are these delicate little meatballs flavored with raisins and nutmeg.

INGREDIENTS

3 ounces ground lean veal
3 ounces ground fairly lean beef
2 teaspoons Your Own Freezer
  Parsley (see page 240)
2 pinches *each* nutmeg and salt
1 slice wheat-germ bread
2 tablespoons milk
2 tablespoons seedless raisins
1 beaten egg
3 tablespoons vegetable oil

ASSEMBLE

small bowl
set measuring spoons
2 cups
chopping knife
fork
medium-sized skillet

DIRECTIONS

Place chopped meats, parsley, salt and nutmeg in bowl. Crumble bread into one cup, cover with milk, then squeeze out the bread and add it to the ingredients in the bowl. Soak raisins in ¾ cup water for 2 minutes. Drain raisins and chop coarsely. Add beaten egg and chopped raisins to bowl. Mix ingredients in bowl lightly with fingers or fork. Gently shape mixture into balls less than one inch in diameter. Heat the oil in the skillet and brown the meatballs on all sides over medium flame. Serve hot.

MELT-IN-YOUR-MOUTH CHEESE BALLS

INGREDIENTS
1 egg white
10 tablespoons grated Cheddar
   or Swiss cheese
3 tablespoons wheat germ
¾ cup vegetable oil

ASSEMBLE
eggbeater or wire whisk
bowl
set measuring spoons
mixing spoon
saucer
skillet
slotted spoon
paper towels

DIRECTIONS
Beat the egg white lightly. Measure the cheese into the bowl and mix in just enough egg white to make a stiff paste. Shape into ¾-inch balls and roll in wheat germ. Fry in hot oil until golden brown on all sides. Remove from oil with a slotted spoon, drain briefly on paper towels and serve immediately.

Soups supreme

Hot and cold

Soup is the most maligned member of all the courses in the family of foods. And the most wonderful! Anyone who calls soup dull, ordinary, unglamorous or any other ugly-duckling name is mistaken. Beautiful soup would be more like it. Warm soup. Comforting soup. Even clever soup. Wise soup. Magic soup. What other food is almost always served in the same form—liquid—and yet manages to conceal within its sameness such differences of taste? Such subtleties of flavor transformed from turnips or carrots or lemons or cabbages into liquids. Disguised. Hidden like secrets in the depths of the bowl. Secrets willing to be discovered if the sipper will but take the time. Puzzles created over hundreds of years. Sometimes complex. Sometimes so simple that only a drop of this or a sprinkle of that can make the difference. This is the languid spot in the meal, the teaser after the invitation, the promise of the hors d'oeuvre. It should be a combination of tastes that lead away from the first course and into the main course, usually with a little something of both hidden in it. Sip, don't gulp. Walk, don't run to the nearest main course. And while you're here . . . enjoy it.

CURRIED LEMON SOUP*

One of the most beautiful soups in the world! From the soft yellow color to the lovely lemon flavor, this soup is lovely, cool impressive, delicious!

INGREDIENTS

1 10½-ounce can cream of
   chicken soup
1 cup light cream
2 teaspoons curry powder
3 tablespoons prepared lemon
   juice

ASSEMBLE

can opener
measuring cup
blender
set measuring spoons
spoon
paring knife
2 soup plates

DIRECTIONS

Open chicken soup and pour into blender. Measure 2 tablespoons of cream into cup, add curry powder and mix well. Fill cup with remaining cream and add to blender. Cover. Blend at high speed for one minute. Stir lemon juice into soup.* Pour soup into bowls over an ice cube. Serve immediately.

GARNISH *(Optional)*

Slice 2 thin slices of lemon. Top each slice with a blanched almond with tiny mint leaves on either side.

* If preparing in advance, omit lemon until immediately before garnishing. Garnish immediately before serving.

FRENCH ONION SOUP*

This it it—practically the national dish of France and the heart's delight of Francophiles everywhere. Real savory, golden-brown onion soup guaranteed to make your guests say "The best I ever tasted," now yours to make in mere minutes. Bon appétit!

INGREDIENTS

3 tablespoons butter

2 small onions, or one medium-sized one

1 tablespoon flour

1 10½-ounce can beef consommé

½ soup can water

1 tablespoon olive oil

½ clove garlic, peeled and crushed

2 slices French bread

6 tablespoons grated Swiss cheese

ASSEMBLE

skillet (medium-sized)

skillet (small)

paring knife

set measuring spoons

fork for stirring

can opener

2 individual flameproof soup servers

DIRECTIONS

Melt 2 tablespoons of butter in a medium-sized skillet. Peel onions and slice thinly. Sauté onions in butter over medium-high heat until they are soft. Stir occasionally to keep from browning. Sprinkle with flour, and stir. Add consommé and water. Stir and bring to a boil. Boil for one minute.

Meanwhile, heat the remaining tablespoon butter, olive oil, and garlic in the small skillet. Cut 2 slices of French bread and fry them in this mixture. Place one slice of bread in the bottom of each serving bowl. Divide the hot onion soup evenly between the two soup servers. Sprinkle each with 3 tablespoons grated Swiss cheese and serve immediately.

* If preparing in advance, reserve garlic bread slices and Swiss cheese. Refrigerate soup until shortly before serving time. Several minutes before serving time, heat soup and continue recipe.

CREAM OF ASPARAGUS SOUP WITH ASPARAGUS TIPS AND ANCHOVY CROUTONS

You won't believe asparagus soup can taste so good! The mellow flavor of creamed asparagus is superbly set off by spicy anchovy croutons. And the treasure in the bottom of the bowl? Asparagus, of course.

INGREDIENTS

1 10½-ounce can cream of
  asparagus soup
½ cup heavy cream
milk (optional)
8 canned asparagus tips
2 slices bread, preferably two
  days old
2 teaspoons anchovy paste
4 tablespoons butter
1 clove garlic, peeled and
  crushed

ASSEMBLE

saucepan
measuring cup
can opener
paring knife
set measuring spoons
skillet
egg beater
2 soup plates

DIRECTIONS

Mix together with eggbeater cream of asparagus soup and heavy cream. If thinner soup is preferred, add a small amount of milk. Place on low heat. Open can of asparagus tips. Drain. Place 8 tips in saucepan with the soup.

Meanwhile, cut away and discard the crusts from the bread, spread bread with anchovy paste and cut into one-inch squares. Melt butter in skillet. Add garlic and sauté bread cubes in the butter until golden. Pour the asparagus soup into the 2 serving bowls. Place 4 asparagus tips in the bottom of each bowl (be careful to keep the tips whole). Place anchovy croutons in a small bowl and spoon into soup at table. Serve hot.

POTATO-CORN CLAM CHOWDER

If there is a soup more hearty or delicious than clam chowder it is Potato-Corn Clam Chowder. This is perfect when served with a New England dinner or on its own as a wonderfully warming lunch.

INGREDIENTS

4 slices bacon
1 10½-ounce can cream of
　potato soup
1 8-ounce can creamed corn
1 7½-ounce can minced clams
1 cup light cream
1 cup milk
½ garlic clove, peeled and
　crushed
2 teaspoons butter
1 or 2 dashes paprika

ASSEMBLE

medium-size saucepan
can opener
paring knife
set measuring spoons
2 soup plates

DIRECTIONS

Cut bacon strips into quarters. Place in bottom of saucepan. Fry over medium heat until cooked but not crisp. Remove from flame. Add potato soup, creamed corn and minced clams to pan (spoon clams in carefully so as not to disturb any sand that might be in the bottom of the can). Add cream, milk, and garlic to pan. Stir. Cook over medium heat until scalding but not boiling. Ladle soup into soup plates. Top each bowl with one teaspoon butter and a dash of paprika. Serve immediately.

NOTE

Serves 4 to 6 and reheats beautifully.

JELLIED MADRILENE IN AVOCADO SHELLS

More than an hors d'oeuvre, more than a soup, this dish can very easily take the place of both. Easy cooking has never been more tasty!

INGREDIENTS
1 avocado
2 teaspoons chilled French
  dressing
1 12½-ounce can jellied
  madrilène, chilled
16 drops lemon juice
2 heaping tablespoons sour cream
4 fresh mint leaves, if available

ASSEMBLE
paring knife
can opener
tablespoon
set measuring spoons
2 serving plates

DIRECTIONS
Cut avocado in half lengthwise. Carefully remove seed and pull off peel. If in a super-hurry, avocado may be left unpeeled. Place one teaspoon French dressing in each avocado shell. Open jellied madrilène. Stir once with tablespoon. Immediately heap jellied madrilène into the hollows of the avocados. Sprinkle each with 8 drops lemon juice.

GARNISH
Top jellied madrilène with one tablespoon of sour cream garnished with 2 mint leaves.

GAZPACHO*

Looking for a soup that's cool, delectable, and a show-stopper as well? Gazpacho's your dish. Serve frosty bowls of tomato-beef broth with mounds of chopped fresh vegetables for your guests to add as they wish.

INGREDIENTS
1 cup cold tomato juice
1 cup cold consommé
2 ice cubes
6 drops Tabasco sauce
4 tablespoons olive oil
¼ teaspoon salt
3 tablespoons prepared lemon
   juice
3 small cloves garlic, peeled
1 large tomato
5 scallions
1 medium-sized cucumber
½ cup Your Own Freezer Green
   Pepper (see page 235)
   uncooked

ASSEMBLE
blender (if not available mix
   with egg beater)
paring knife
measuring cup
set measuring spoons
garlic press
set of garlic press
set of small bowls
2 soup plates

DIRECTIONS
Place in blender tomato juice, consommé, Tabasco sauce, olive oil, salt, lemon juice and garlic. Cover blender. Turn on high speed for one minute. Meanwhile, wash tomato and scallions. Peel cucumber. Chop tomato, cucumber, and scallions the size of your thumbnail. Place all vegetables in individual bowls.*

* May be prepared to this point several hours in advance of serving. Place in refrigerator until serving time. Blend slightly before proceeding with recipe.

Place ice cubes in serving bowls. Pour soup over ice cubes. Serve immediately. Pass bowls of vegetables.

GARNISH *(Optional)*
Top each bowl of soup with finely chopped parsley and one very thin slice unpeeled cucumber.

CHILLY CRÈME DE MENTHE SOUP

A soup fascinating in its unusual flavor. Smoky and minty at the same time. Creamy, deliciously cool.

INGREDIENTS

⅓ 11-ounce can split green pea soup (with ham)

⅓ 10½-ounce can cream of celery soup

⅓ 10½-ounce can cream of chicken soup

3 ice cubes, cracked

a pinch of garlic powder

a pinch of thyme

1 teaspoon parsley flakes

3 tablespoons water

1 cup light cream

2 tablespoons crème de menthe

ASSEMBLE

blender (if not available mix soup in a bowl and strain)

measuring cup

tablespoon

set measuring spoons

2 soup plates

DIRECTIONS

Place soups in blender with thyme, garlic powder and ice cubes. Add parsley flakes and water. Blend on high speed for one minute. Turn off blender. Add light cream to blender mixture. Blend on low for 10 seconds more. Add crème de menthe. Blend on low speed for 10 seconds. Pour into soup plates. Serve cold.

May also be served without crème de menthe, either hot or cold.

GARNISH *(Optional)*

Serve with a dollop of whipped cream in the center of the soup. Tuck 3 fresh mint leaves slightly under the whipped cream. Serve immediately.

GARLIC SOUP WITH CROUTONS AND POACHED EGG*

Soupophiles, be sure to try this epicure's delight. Steaming garlicky beef broth, tender poached egg, and garlic croutons surely make this a treat in itself as well as a harbinger of good things to come.

INGREDIENTS

¼ cup good-quality olive
  oil
1 clove garlic, peeled
20 ready-made croutons or bread
  squares
1 10½-ounce can beef
  consommé
¾ soup can water
dash each salt, pepper, and
  paprika
2 eggs
2 thin slices tomato

ASSEMBLE

large skillet
can opener
slotted spoon
paring knife
fine strainer
2 soup plates

DIRECTIONS

Place the skillet over medium heat. Add olive oil. Crush garlic over pan and heat until oil is smoking hot. Add croutons or bread cubes and fry for one minute. Turn often. Remove croutons from pan with slotted spoon. Add consommé, water, and paprika to pan and bring to a boil. When boiling, turn flame down until liquid is barely bubbling. Break eggs into liquid. Be careful not to break yolks. Spoon liquid over eggs until they are cooked (about 3 minutes). Remove eggs with slotted spoon carefully and place one in each serving dish. Strain consommé into bowls over eggs. Sprinkle with salt, pepper, and paprika. Add croutons and tomato slices. Serve instantly.

GARNISH *(Optional)*
Sprinkle with finely chopped fresh parsley before serving.

* To prepare in advance, make croutons and keep at room temperature. Make soup and refrigerate. Shortly before serving, heat soup to steaming, add eggs, and continue as above.

TOMATO CRAB BISQUE

If there were only one soup in the whole world, all would be well if it was Tomato Crab Bisque. Pale tomato in color, delicately textured, it's replete with the unforgettable flavor of crabmeat and sherry. Serve only for V.I.P.s—and for yourself, of course.

INGREDIENTS

½ 10¾-ounce can cream of
tomato soup
½ 10½-ounce can beef
consommé
½ 11¼-ounce can split pea soup
(without ham)
½ cup light cream
½ pound crabmeat (frozen)
½ cup sherry

ASSEMBLE

large saucepan
egg beater
tablespoon
measuring cup
can opener
2 soup plates

DIRECTIONS

Mix the soups together in the saucepan. Use no water. Add cream and beat with the eggbeater until well mixed. Remove shells from crabmeat by picking through it with fingers and discarding anything that feels hard. Put the crabmeat in the soup mixture and heat until steaming. Do not boil. Add sherry a little at a time. Ladle into serving bowls. Serve hot.

GARNISH *(Optional)*

Chop 2 tablespoons parsley and sprinkle over center of soup. Sprinkle the outer edges of the soup with paprika. Serve hot.

CREAMY COD CHOWDER

*This is perhaps the most delectable fish chowder ever! Serve it
before a simple dinner or with homebaked bread and a salad
for an unusually pleasing lunch.*

INGREDIENTS
½ pound cod fillet
1 10¾-ounce can chicken
   broth
1 tablespoon butter
1 tablespoon cooking oil
1 medium-sized tomato, seeded
   and chopped
1 clove garlic, peeled and
   crushed
1 tablespoon flour
⅛ teaspoon ground nutmeg
⅔ cup heavy cream
2 slices French bread, fried in
   olive oil (optional)
dash of paprika

ASSEMBLE
large sharp knife
2 medium-sized skillets
can opener
garlic press
set measuring spoons
measuring cup
stirring spoon
small skillet
soup ladle

DIRECTIONS
Quickly cut the fish into one-inch cubes, discarding any bone.
Place the fish and the chicken broth in a skillet and bring to a
boil over high heat. Lower the heat to medium and boil for 8
minutes.

Meanwhile, heat the butter and cooking oil in the second skillet, add the onion, tomato and garlic, then sauté for 4 minutes.
Stir in the flour and nutmeg. Add the heavy cream all at once

and cook over medium heat, stirring constantly, until the sauce is thick and bubbling. Sauté the bread slices in olive oil until golden brown, turning once.

Stir the hot vegetable sauce into the fish and chicken broth until well blended. Place one sautéed bread slice in each soup bowl. Ladle the soup over the bread, sprinkle with paprika and serve immediately.

SPICY SPINACH SOUP WITH CHICKPEAS

If a really zesty soup is your choice, do try this one. A crunchy loaf of French bread, a bar of sweet butter, and a wedge of cheese will transform this hearty soup into a full meal.

INGREDIENTS

1 medium-sized onion, peeled and chopped
1 clove garlic, peeled and crushed
2 tablespoons olive oil
1 10-ounce package frozen chopped spinach, defrosted
1 10¾-ounce can chicken broth
¼ teaspoon thyme
½ 20-ounce can chickpeas, drained
2 hard-cooked eggs, shelled and chopped

ASSEMBLE

sharp knife
garlic press
medium-sized skillet
can opener
colander

DIRECTIONS

Sauté the onion and garlic in the olive oil for 3 minutes. Add the spinach and chicken broth. Add chickpeas to the soup. Stir in thyme. Cook over medium heat until the spinach is done. Garnish each portion with chopped egg and serve immediately.

SQUASH SOUP ELEGANT

There has never been a soup more ambrosial than this one. Delicate yet rich, delightful served hot or cold—this soup is truly in a class by itself.

INGREDIENTS
1 12-ounce package frozen puréed winter squash, defrosted
1 10¾-ounce can chicken broth
⅛ teaspoon garlic salt (or ½ small garlic clove, peeled and crushed)
3 tablespoons heavy cream
1 tablespoon sherry
sprinkle of nutmeg
2 teaspoons sour cream

ASSEMBLE
can opener
medium-sized enamel or glass saucepan
stirring spoon
set measuring spoons
wire whisk or eggbeater
soup ladle

DIRECTIONS
Mix together the squash, chicken broth and garlic in the saucepan. Cook over high flame for 8 minutes, stirring occasionally. Skim the foam from the top of the soup, then beat in the heavy cream and the sherry. Sprinkle the soup with nutmeg before serving hot or cold, garnished with one teaspoon of sour cream in the center of each bowl.

The entrée

Supreme moment of the meal

As elegant and enticing as your hors d'oeuvre has been, as soothing and full of promise as your soup has been, still these have been but a prologue leading to the main attraction—the entrée. Thus far in your meal you have hinted at what was to come—made beautiful promises. Now the time has arrived to make those promises good. The main course must live up to the expectations of your guests, magic *you* have led them to expect by the perfection of your first two courses.

Does that sound like a challenge? It is! But one you can handle with ease. There is nothing chancy about a perfect meal. It must be planned and executed with care. Quick does not mean haphazard! A meal should be planned with the entrée as its peak. Choose your main course first, then build out on either side.

Pick up a spice in your main event and repeat it, subtly, in your soup. Isolate a texture or a flavor or even a color and extend it in a way complementary to your entrée.

It's just a matter of *thinking* about your foods as the individual personalities that they are. Select your foods as carefully as you select your friends and vice versa, and your reputation as a cook as well as your reputation as a hostess will soar.

SHRIMPS FLAMBÉ

Shrimp with a flourish! Exciting to look at, even more exciting to eat, and what oohs and aahs when you perform your cookery right at the table!

INGREDIENTS
5 tablespoons butter
16 very large cleaned, uncooked
    shrimp, available at your fish
    store
1 clove garlic, peeled and
    crushed
¼ cup applejack or apple brandy
¼ cup heavy cream
¼ teaspoon nutmeg
1 tablespoon Your Own Freezer
    Chives (see page 239)

ASSEMBLE
chafing dish
Sterno
tablespoon
set measuring spoons
measuring cup
small saucepan

DIRECTIONS
Light flame under blazer pan of chafing dish. Melt butter. Add shrimp and garlic, then cook over high heat for 3 minutes. Remove from flame. Heat the applejack in the small saucepan. Pour gently over shrimp and light with a match. When brandy burns out, cook over high flame for 2 minutes. Add cream and nutmeg. Stir until hot. Sprinkle with chopped chives. Serve hot, either alone or over toast points or rice.

NOTE
This entire process may be performed at the table or, if desired, while still in kitchen bring recipe to the point where brandy is added and continue from this point before guests.

WINE
Pouilly-Fuissé or other dry white wine, slightly chilled

BOUILLABAISSE
(serves 4)

A zesty and potent dark golden fish stew—A humble soup glorified by gourmets the world round—A fisherman's child turned king of the table, bouillabaisse reigns as the world's favorite fish dish.

INGREDIENTS

2 10½-ounce cans consommé
10 ounces clam juice
16 tablespoons tomato sauce or 5
  tablespoons tomato paste
1 cup frozen or canned
  chopped carrots
1 cup Your Own Freezer Onions
  (see page 237)
2 cloves garlic, peeled and crushed
4 teaspoons Your Own Freezer
  Parsley (see page 240)
½ teaspoon fennel seeds
½ teaspoon thyme
2 small bay leaves
1½ teaspoons saffron
4 tablespoons frozen
  concentrated orange juice
1½ teaspoons instant coffee
½ pound tail end of cod
½ pound fillet of flounder
½ pound red snapper
½ pound eel
16 frozen shrimp, cleaned and
  shelled

ASSEMBLE

large pot
tablespoon
nutcracker
sharp knife
cooking spoon
paper towels
can opener
set measuring spoons
2 soup plates

1 whole cooked lobster in shell,
   cut in 1-inch pieces
3 tablespoons vegetable oil or
   butter
2 tablespoons Pernod
1 3¾-ounce can king crabmeat
(If any of the above are not available,
   replace with a similar variety
   of fish.)
2 teaspoons anchovy paste
½ cup olive oil
2 slices Your Own Freezer
   Garlic Toasts (see page 244)

DIRECTIONS
In a large, heavy pot sauté lobster and shrimp briefly in butter.
Add Pernod and set aflame.

Put consommé and clam juice in pot and bring to a boil over
high heat. Add tomato sauce (or tomato paste), vegetables,
garlic, parsley, fennel seeds, thyme, bay leaves, saffron, frozen
orange juice concentrate, instant coffee, anchovy paste, and
olive oil. Continue to boil while you cut fish into ¾-inch slices.
Place cod slices and frozen shrimp in pot.

Remove claws from lobster. Crack slightly with nutcracker.
Add lobster and claws to pot. Place flounder pieces on top of
boiling soup. Cook for 4 minutes. Meanwhile heat 2 frozen garlic
toasts in skillet. Place one slice in each soup plate. Stir crabmeat
into soup and ladle soup over bread.

WINE
Pouilly-Fuissé or other dry white wine, slightly chilled

FISH WITH BEER AND GINGERSNAPS

If you're looking for a main course that is different to the point of being adventurous, serve this! Luscious white fish swimming in a sauce of sparkling dark beer, its flavor sweetened and heightened with gingersnaps. Not everyone's plate of fish, but definitely a winner.

INGREDIENTS

2 fillets of flounder
¼ teaspoon salt
1 cup dark beer
1 bay leaf
½ teaspoon lemon juice
¼ teaspoon sugar
3 gingersnaps
1½ teaspoons flour
1 tablespoon butter

ASSEMBLE

large skillet
set measuring spoons
paring knife
measuring cup
spoon
small mixing bowl
paper towels

DIRECTIONS

Wash fish and sprinkle with salt. Place one cup dark beer (to measure beer allow foam to settle slightly), bay leaf, and the fish in the skillet with the lemon juice and sugar. Cook over medium high heat. If fish begins to break up, reduce heat to low. Meanwhile, remove 4 tablespoons of the fish-beer liquid and place in mixing bowl with gingersnaps. Add flour and butter to this. Mash with spoon until fairly smooth. Remove fish from liquid and keep warm. Add mixture in mixing bowl to that in the skillet. Cook over high heat, stirring constantly, until slightly thickened. Serve hot with several tablespoons sauce over each portion fish.

GARNISH *(Optional)*
Serve with 2 sprigs of parsley under 2 thin slices of lemon. Top
lemon with small crisscross of pimiento slices. Serve immediately.

WINE
Dry Rhine, slightly chilled

SHRIMP CURRY

Here's a heavenly curry cooked with coconut milk for a taste
surprise. Different but divine, and a real reputation builder, too!

INGREDIENTS
1 4-ounce can shredded coconut
2½ cups milk
16 large cooked and cleaned
   shrimp, available at your fish
   store
3 tablespoons butter
1 teaspoon salt
2 tablespoons flour
1½ tablespoons curry powder
1 cup Your Own Freezer Rice
   (see page 242)

ASSEMBLE
2 saucepans (6-cup)
skillet
strainer
2 spoons
colander
measuring cup
measuring spoons

DIRECTIONS
Put the shredded coconut and the milk in one saucepan. Heat.
until scalding but do not boil. In the other pan place the shrimp
and 2 cups of hot water. Let stand until shrimp are hot. Meanwhile, melt butter in frying pan. Add salt and flour and stir
until smooth. Add the curry powder and again stir until

smooth. Use the strainer to drain the milk from the coconut. Retain both. Pour milk into butter and flour mixture. Stir constantly over medium high flame until this begins to bubble and thicken. Cook for one minute more. Drain shrimp in colander. Pour curry sauce into serving bowl. Decorate with shrimp and shredded coconut. Serve hot with rice.

NOTE
This recipe serves 2 generously. To serve 3, add 8 large shrimp *only*. To serve 4, double entire recipe.

WINE
Bordeaux Graves or other dry white wine, slightly chilled

ESCARGOTS BOURGUIGNONNE
(Snails Burgundy)

Succulent snails in the traditional garlic sauce—the classic of French gourmet cooking! Fabulous for that really special occasion.

INGREDIENTS

1 7½-ounce can snails with package of snail shells
5 tablespoons cognac
2 cloves garlic, peeled and crushed
¼ teaspoon salt
¼ pound cold butter
2 tablespoons each Your Own Freezer Parsley (see page 240) and Your Own Freezer Chives (see page 239)

ASSEMBLE

can opener
set measuring spoons
strainer
small pan
2 tablespoons
dish towel
mixing bowl
flat flameproof dish or pan

DIRECTIONS

Light broiler and set on high. Drain snails in strainer. Heat snails, cognac, salt, and half the garlic over medium high flame. Meanwhile, in the mixing bowl mash butter with a spoon. Add the remaining garlic, parsley leaves, and chopped chives, and mix thoroughly with the butter. Place ¼ teaspoon of butter mixture in each of the snail shells. Drain the snails again in strainer. Add one snail to each of the snail shells. Use the rest of the butter mixture to seal the openings of the snail shells. Place the filled snail shells on the flat flameproof dish or pan. Heat under the broiler for 3 minutes. Serve very hot.

WINE

Bordeaux Graves or other dry white wine, slightly chilled

SHRIMP SCAMPI

You'll never believe this gourmet standby is so easy to prepare. Large succulent shrimp swimming in sputtering hot garlic-butter sauce—really delightful!

INGREDIENTS
14 very large shrimp or prawns, raw
¼ cup olive oil
3 tablespoons butter
3 cloves garlic, crushed
1 tablespoon parsley flakes
¼ teaspoon salt

ASSEMBLE
pair scissors
paper towels
garlic press
measuring cup
set measuring spoons
skillet
2 serving plates

DIRECTIONS
Remove shell from shrimp and clean by making a ¼-inch cut with scissors down the middle of the round back. Remove the vein down center of back. Wash in cold water and place each shrimp, as it is cleaned, on paper towels to drain. Place skillet over high flame. Add olive oil and butter. Add shrimp and cook about 3 minutes, stirring frequently. Add garlic pulp to contents of skillet along with parsley and salt. Cook for one minute more. Stir several times. Place seven shrimp on each plate. Divide sauce evenly. Serve very hot.

WINE
Pouilly-Fuissé or other dry white wine, slightly chilled

DANISH FISH WITH BLUE CHEESE

Pearly white halibut in a luscious piquant blue cheese sauce. A gourmet's delight and so amazingly easy to prepare.

INGREDIENTS	ASSEMBLE
2 slices fresh halibut, not too thick	paper towels
	skillet
½ teaspoon salt	tablespoon
4 tablespoons butter	paring knife
½ cup Danish blue cheese	set measuring spoons
1 tablespoon lemon juice	fork
2 wedges of lemon	flameproof dish for broiling
2 sprigs parsley	and serving

DIRECTIONS

Turn broiler flame on high. Wash fish, blot with paper towels and rub with salt. Place several small pieces of butter in the broiling dish. Arrange fish over these and put under broiler flame. Melt the remaining butter in the skillet. Stir in blue cheese and lemon juice. Baste fish with this mixture. Continue cooking until fish flakes when pricked with a fork, or about 7 minutes. Decorate fish with lemon wedges and sprigs of parsley. Serve hot.

WINE

Pouilly-Fuissé or other dry white wine, slightly chilled

CALF'S LIVER PARIS

If you are convinced that there is only one way to prepare liver and that is fried with bacon, this recipe should be a revelation to you. Thin slices of that lovely liver, perfectly combined with shallots, nutmeg, and white wine—and not a slice of bacon in sight. Leave it to the Parisennes.

INGREDIENTS

4 very thin slices of calf's liver
6 tablespoons butter
4 whole shallots, peeled, washed, and chopped
¾ cup dry white wine
1 pinch nutmeg
1 tablespoon lemon juice
4 sprigs parsley, washed and chopped
1 egg yolk
2 large pinches of salt

ASSEMBLE

large skillet
medium-size skillet
set measuring spoons
measuring cup
paring knife
fork
paper towels
serving plate

DIRECTIONS

Wash liver slices and blot with paper towels. Melt butter in medium skillet. Add shallots to butter in pan. Cook for one minute over high flame. Add the wine and the nutmeg, and continue to cook over high heat for 2 minutes more. Add the lemon juice and turn flame very low. In large skillet quickly sear the liver slices on both sides over high heat. Remove from pan and keep warm. Beat egg yolk and add to sauce with salt. Stir until slightly thickened. Place the liver slices on serving dish and cover with the sauce. Sprinkle with chopped parsley and serve immediately.

GARNISH *(Optional)*
Place 5 or 6 cherry tomatoes in skillet with 2 tablespoons butter. Cook over medium heat for a few minutes. Arrange cherry tomatoes a few inches apart around edge of dish. Tuck whole parsley leaves beside each tomato. Serve hot.

WINE
Beaujolais

BREAST OF CHICKEN IN RUM CRUMBS

A warm buttery delight! A crusty "sandwich" where chicken slices sautéed in rum crumbs are the "bread" and marrons and chutney form the filling.

INGREDIENTS
2 boneless chicken breasts, each
    split to form large slices,
    ½-inch thick
½ cup fine bread crumbs
¼ cup rum
¼ pound butter
3 marrons glacés
1 tablespoon chutney, with liquid
1 tablespoon rum

ASSEMBLE
small saucepan
sharp knife
large skillet
measuring cup
mallet or meat tenderizer
fork
small bowl
plate (for bread crumbs)
serving plate

DIRECTIONS

Pull skin from chicken. Flatten each slice chicken breast slightly with mallet or fine side of meat tenderizer. Place bread crumbs on plate. Pour ¼ cup rum into small bowl. Dip chicken in rum, then in bread crumbs. Turn flame medium high. Melt butter in skillet. Sauté each chicken slice one minute on each side or until golden. Meanwhile, mash marrons and chutney with one tablespoon rum. Warm in saucepan. Add a few bread crumbs if needed to make mixture spreadable. Spread this on one side of 2 chicken slices. Top with another sautéed chicken slice. Serve hot.

GARNISH *(Optional)*

See recipe for Marrons in Apricots. Tuck a small piece of parsley under each apricot half. Serve hot.

WINE

Beaujolais or Bordeaux Graves, slightly chilled

LOBSTER-SHRIMP OR CRAYFISH IN WINE RICE

One of the most delicate dishes. Bright red-orange lobster-shrimp or crayfish steeped in the most subtle of sauces.

INGREDIENTS

1 cup Your Own Freezer
   Rice (see page 242)
10 lobster-shrimp or crayfish
6 tablespoons butter
1 tablespoon brandy
4 shallots
2 tablespoons chopped parsley
large pinch of thyme
2 tablespoons tomato sauce
1 bay leaf
1 cup dry white wine
6 tablespoons heavy cream
1/4 teaspoon salt

ASSEMBLE

scissors
medium saucepan
large skillet
set measuring spoons
measuring cup
colander
paring knife
paper towels
serving dish

DIRECTIONS

Prepare rice according to directions. Meanwhile, make 1/4-inch cut with scissors in round backs of crayfish, remove vein and wash in colander. Do not remove shells. Turn onto paper towels to drain.

Melt butter in skillet. Sauté crayfish for one minute over high heat, turning them once. Pour brandy over the mixture in the skillet. Flame the brandy with a match held close to the crayfish. Continue to cook over low flame while you peel and chop shallots and parsley. Add shallots, parsley, thyme, tomato sauce, bay leaf, and wine to skillet. Boil over high flame for 2 minutes. Stir in cream. Arrange rice and shrimp on serving dish. Pour sauce over rice. Serve hot.

GARNISH *(Optional)*
Tuck pieces of fresh parsley in among the crayfish. Peel and chop a black truffle and cook it in a little white wine for one minute. Drain truffle and sprinkle over lobster-shrimp and rice in serving bowl.

WINE
Pouilly-Fuissé or other dry white wine, slightly chilled

SUKIYAKI

If you are tired of Chinese food, try Japanese. Sukiyaki has the excitement of the East about it, but in a different, more delicate way. Picture firm, yet tender vegetables and succulent thin beef slices, gently cooked in sweet salt beef broth and served on small mountains of pearly rice. Fabulous!

INGREDIENTS

1 cup Your Own Freezer Rice
  (see page 242)
1 medium-sized onion
4 large mushrooms
½ pound thin-sliced rare roast
  beef, available at any
  delicatessen
¼ pound fresh spinach
4 scallions
3 five-inch pieces celery
½ 10½-ounce can beef
  consommé
4 tablespoons soy sauce
2 tablespoons sugar
3 tablespoons vegetable oil

ASSEMBLE

saucepan
iron skillet or other heavy
  skillet
paper towels
spoon
colander
set measuring spoons
paring knife
can opener
measuring cup

DIRECTIONS

Prepare rice according to directions. Place skillet on medium flame. Meanwhile, peel onion and mushrooms. Slice. Add oil, onion, mushrooms, and roast beef to skillet. In colander, wash spinach, scallions, and celery. Turn onto paper towels to drain. Quickly slice spinach into one-inch pieces. Slice celery and scallions diagonally. Add to skillet. Add soy sauce, sugar, and consommé to skillet. Stir. Cook for 2 minutes. Stir again. Serve hot over the rice. (The Japanese serve each guest with a small bowl containing one raw, beaten egg into which each forkful may be dipped prior to eating. Try it.)

LOBSTER PERNOD OR ABSINTHE GOURMET

Combine the exotic flavors of lobster, chervil, white wine and Pernod (or absinthe) in one steaming caldron and people will sit up and take notice!

INGREDIENTS

3 small lobsters, cooked. Available at your fish store. Ask to have them cut, shell and all, into 2-inch slices
1 cup white wine
1 tablespoon flour
3 tablespoons butter
¼ teaspoon salt
⅛ teaspoon white pepper
1 tablespoon dried tarragon
1½ tablespoons dried chervil
¼ cup Pernod (or absinthe)

ASSEMBLE

kettle
saucepan
set measuring spoons
measuring cup
butcher knife
nutcracker (pincher type)
spoon
serving dish
serving ladle

DIRECTIONS

Discard heads of lobsters; crack claws with nutcracker. Place pieces of lobster in kettle. Cover with one cup of white wine. Measure flour, 2 tablespoons butter, salt and pepper into saucepan. Stir until butter melts and sauce is slightly thickened. Add tarragon, chervil and remaining tablespoon butter to lobster meat. When hot add Pernod or absinthe and set aflame. After flame dies add butter sauce. Bring to a boil, stirring constantly. Serve hot.

WINE

Pouilly-Fuissé or other dry white wine, slightly chilled

BOEUF AU VIN BLANC

A lovely blend of beef and butter, shallots and white wine. Not overstated, not understated: just perfectly Parisienne.

INGREDIENTS
2 shallots
2 tablespoons Your Own Freezer
   Onions (see page 237)
1/4 teaspoon salt
1/8 teaspoon coarse black pepper
3 tablespoons butter
1 pound sliced rare roast beef,
   available at any delicatessen
1/3 cup white wine
5 tablespoons beef consommé
1 clove garlic
3 tablespoons Your Own Freezer
   Parsley (see page 240)

ASSEMBLE
medium-sized skillet
measuring cup
set measuring spoons
paring knife
can opener
garlic press
serving dish

DIRECTIONS
Place onion, shallots, salt and pepper, butter and meat in skillet. Cook for 2 minutes over high heat. Meanwhile, measure wine and consommé. Add to skillet along with crushed garlic and chopped parsley. Cook over high heat until sauce barely covers meat. Serve hot.

GARNISH
Finely chop 2 sprigs parsley. Sprinkle over beef. Serve immediately.

WINE
Pomerol (Bordeaux)

KIDNEYS FLAMBÉ

Rich and delicious as only kidneys can be. Top them with bacon, shallots, mushrooms, and truffles (not to mention brandy and cream), and you won't believe what a marvelous cook you are.

INGREDIENTS

3 strips bacon
3 veal kidneys
2 scallions
2 tablespoons Your Own Freezer
   Shallots (see page 239)
¾ cup Your Own Freezer
   Mushrooms (see page 243)
2 tablespoons butter
2 black truffles
¼ teaspoon salt
1 large pinch coarse black
   pepper
5 tablespoons heavy cream
2 tablespoons brandy

ASSEMBLE

chafing dish
Sterno
paring knife
set measuring spoons
stirring spoon
serving plate

DIRECTIONS

Place bacon in blazer pan of chafing dish. Cook over low flame. Cut kidneys into thin slices. Discard fat and membrane. Wash, trim, and thinly slice scallions and truffles. Sauté kidneys in the bacon fat for one minute over high flame. Add scallions, shallots, mushrooms, butter, truffles, salt, and pepper to skillet. Cook over medium heat for 2 minutes. Add heavy cream to mixture in skillet. Stir. Pour brandy over kidneys. When warm, set aflame. Serve hot.

GARNISH *(Optional)*
Alongside of serving dish place half broiled tomato. Place several leaves of watercress under each. Tuck small sprigs of watercress 2 inches apart around side of dish. Serve immediately.

WINE
Bordeaux Graves

SPAGHETTI WITH WHITE CLAM SAUCE

Breathes there the fine Italian restaurant that doesn't brag about its linguine? No, it's true they do, and rightly. Now you can, too!

INGREDIENTS

3 tablespoons olive oil
¼ pound butter
1 4-ounce can minced clams, or
  1 dozen fresh clams, chopped
1 tablespoon Your Own Freezer
  Parsley (see page 240)
¼ teaspoon salt
¼ teaspoon Tabasco sauce
2 cloves garlic, peeled and
  crushed
1 8-ounce box spaghetti or
  linguine
2 quarts boiling water
2 tablespoons oregano
⅛ teaspoon coarsely ground
  black pepper

ASSEMBLE

kettle or large pot
set measuring spoons
can opener
garlic press
medium-sized skillet
colander

DIRECTIONS

Place skillet over medium heat. Add olive oil, butter, clams (spoon clams and liquid into pan so as not to disturb sand which may be in the bottom of container), parsley, salt, Tabasco sauce and garlic. Cook until mixture begins to bubble. Meantime cook spaghetti al dente in boiling water according to directions on package, and drain. Place spaghetti in large serving dish and pour sauce over it. Sprinkle with oregano and black pepper. Toss spaghetti and sauce together at table. Serve immediately.

WINE

Orvieto Secco or other Italian dry white wine, slightly chilled

HAM PARMENTIER

Leftover ham takes on a new dimension when combined with rich, creamy sauce and heaped on thick slices of Italian bread.

INGREDIENTS

1 cup Your Own Freezer Onion
  (see page 237)
1 cup Your Own Freezer Green
  Pepper (see page 235)
2 tablespoons butter
8 large mushrooms
1 cup leftover cooked chopped
  ham
1 tablespoon cooking oil
2 center slices Italian bread
1 teaspoon all-purpose flour
3/4 cup heavy cream
1 tablespoon Worcestershire sauce
1 teaspoon Dijon mustard
2 hard-cooked eggs, sliced
4 sprigs watercress, washed

ASSEMBLE

medium-sized skillet
sharp knife (chopping)
stirring spoon
small skillet
measuring cup
set measuring spoons

DIRECTIONS

Sauté the onion and green pepper in the butter for 2 minutes. Meanwhile, coarsely chop the mushrooms. Add the mushrooms and ham to the pan and cook, stirring occasionally, for 3 minutes. In the meantime, place the oil in the smaller skillet and sauté the bread slices until brown on both sides. Keep warm.

Stir the flour into the ham and vegetables, then add the cream all at once along with the Worcestershire sauce and mustard. Stir over medium heat until the sauce is thick. Arrange the sautéed bread on two plates, spoon the ham mixture over and top with the hard-cooked eggs and watercress. Serve immediately.

VEAL BOLOGNESE

Here is quick cooking at its very best—veal scallopine dipped in egg, fried in crumbs and topped with a fresh-tasting, creamy tomato sauce.

INGREDIENTS

2 good-sized pieces veal scallopine
2 tablespoons butter
1 egg
½ cup bread crumbs
4-ounce container Your Own
  Freezer Tomato Purée (see
  page 241)
½ cup heavy cream
pinch each of nutmeg and thyme
salt and pepper to taste
4 sprigs watercress

ASSEMBLE

2 shallow bowls
medium-sized skillet
small saucepan
fork
stirring spoon
2 serving plates

DIRECTIONS

Have your butcher pound the veal very thin. Heat the butter in the skillet. Beat the egg in one of the shallow bowls and place the bread crumbs in the other. Dip each piece of veal first in egg, then in bread crumbs, and fry in the butter to a golden brown on both sides, turning once.

Meanwhile, cook the tomato purée over medium heat for 2 minutes. Stir in the cream and seasonings.

Remove the meat from the pan and set aside to keep warm. Add the tomato-cream mixture to the juices remaining in the skillet. Stir over medium heat for one minute, or until the sauce is fairly thick. Arrange the veal slices on serving plates, spoon the sauce over and serve immediately, garnished with watercress.

WINE
Soave, slightly chilled

SCHNITZEL À LA HOLSTEIN

Veal is perhaps the most elegant of meats, and scallopine is the choicest cut of veal. This outstanding German veal dish features scallopine that is first dipped in egg and bread crumbs and cooked to a glorious golden brown, then topped with a whole fried egg and finally crisscrossed with zesty anchovies.

INGREDIENTS
2 good-sized pieces veal scallopine
3 tablespoons butter
3 eggs
1/2 cup bread crumbs
4 flat anchovy fillets
2 teaspoons capers
2 sprigs parsley

ASSEMBLE
2 medium-sized skillets
2 shallow bowls
fork
spatula
2 serving plates

DIRECTIONS
Have your butcher pound the veal as thin as possible. Heat 2 tablespoons of butter in one skillet. Beat one egg lightly in one of the shallow bowls and place the bread crumbs in the other. Dip each veal piece first in egg, then in bread crumbs, and fry in the butter to a golden brown on both sides, turning once.

Meanwhile, place the remaining butter in the second skillet and fry 2 eggs as you like them (the centers should be soft). Arrange the fried eggs over the meat, crisscross each egg with 2 anchovy fillets, sprinkle with capers, and garnish with parsley. Serve at once.

WINE
Beaujolais (or other light red Burgundy)

Salads

The perfect meal's perfect wife

Nothing is more important to the meal than the salad. Designed to cool the tongue and render it neutral and ready to fully appreciate the next course, the salad has become much more than that.

If the meal is hot and spicy, the salad should be cool and green. If the meal is subtle and rather bland, the salad should be crunchy and tart. If the meal is a foreign or unusual one, the salad should not fight for attention, but rather be an extension of the exotic flavors of the meal. Still, the salad should have character and subtleties within its own flavor structure, cooling the taste buds to prepare them for the next treat, saying, "Wake up! Something good is coming."

At all times the salad should be chosen carefully. In its color, texture, and flavor, whether served before, after, or during the main course, a salad should always beautifully complement the meal it accompanies.

ONION SALAD

At last onions get the special treatment they deserve: a salad of their very own! Two varieties of sweet onions combine with an anchovy dressing to make a salad treat that adds zow to the plainest meal. If you like onions you'll love this.

INGREDIENTS
1 small red onion
1 small sweet Bermuda onion
2 tablespoons wine vinegar
¼ cup olive oil
2 teaspoons anchovy paste
16 pitted black olives
freshly ground black pepper to
   taste

ASSEMBLE
butcher knife
can opener
strainer
measuring cup
set measuring spoons
tablespoon
small mixing bowl
salad bowl

DIRECTIONS
Peel and cut onions into thin slices. Arrange neatly in salad bowl. Refrigerate. Place vinegar, olive oil, and anchovy paste in mixing bowl. Beat vigorously. Drain the black olives. Remove salad bowl from refrigerator, arrange olives on top of onion slices. Stir dressing and pour over salad. Sprinkle with pepper. Serve cold.

LOBSTER SALAD*
(serves 4)

This lobster salad is fit for a king. However, if you aren't expecting any kings, try it out on your favorite guests and prepare to be hailed as a queen among cooks. Lobster, chicken. shrimp, turkey, and ham combine to make this the perfect main-course salad for a luncheon or a late-night snack. Try it also as a stuffing for tomatoes to serve with a cold meal. Delicious!

INGREDIENTS
2 cooked lobsters. Ask to have them split and the claws cracked.
18 large cooked shrimp, available in your fish store
5 heaping tablespoons mayonnaise
1/2 teaspoon salt
2 tablespoons tarragon vinegar
2 tablespoons olive oil
2 level teaspoons mustard
tomalley of lobster, if available
18 stuffed green olives
1/2 pound boiled sliced ham
1/2 pound sliced turkey, available in any delicatessen
3 tablespoons capers, drained
4 leaves of lettuce or escarole

ASSEMBLE
large mixing bowl
set measuring spoons
measuring cup
spoon
2 forks
paring knife
paper towels
4 serving plates

DIRECTIONS

Remove meat from tail section of lobster without breaking shell. Cut into ½-inch slices. Cut 10 shrimps in pieces. Reserve 8 whole shrimp for trim. Place mayonnaise, salt, vinegar, olive oil, mustard, tomalley of lobster, and 10 whole olives in the mixing bowl. Stir. Cut ham and turkey in ½-inch strips. Add strips of ham and turkey, the chopped shrimp and lobster, and capers to mayonnaise mixture. Toss, using the two forks.

GARNISH

Wash lettuce and drain on paper towels. Arrange lettuce leaves on salad plates. Place ½ split lobster on each plate. Mound the salad in the center of each lobster shell. Garnish with whole shrimps and olives. Serve cold.

* May be prepared several hours in advance of serving. Refrigerate.

CUCUMBER SALAD DAMASCUS*

Does the meal you plan cry for something cool and unusually delicious? Then this is the salad at the end of the rainbow for you. Cucumber Salad Damascus has all the requirements necessary to go with the spicy meal. It is cool in texture, flavor, color, and temperature. In other words, it's perfect.

INGREDIENTS
1½ cucumbers, peeled and
   thinly sliced
¼ cup yogurt
½ clove garlic
salt and pepper to taste
2 tablespoons Your Own Freezer
   Chives (see page 239)
1 tablespoon chopped mint

ASSEMBLE
paring knife
measuring cup
set measuring spoons
spoon
garlic press
mixing bowl
tablespoon
salad bowl
salad fork and spoon

DIRECTIONS
Place cucumber slices in mixing bowl. Leave yogurt in measuring cup. Peel and crush garlic. Stir garlic and yogurt together. Sprinkle salt and pepper on cucumbers. Refrigerate yogurt mixture and cucumbers separately.* To serve, drain cucumbers. Toss cucumbers and yogurt mixture together, place in salad bowl and sprinkle with chives and mint. Serve cold.

NOTE
To serve 3, add ½ cucumber. To serve 4, double entire recipe.

* May be prepared an hour in advance of serving. Refrigerate until needed.

CAULIFLOWER SALAD*

An unexpected combination of ingredients makes this a salad of unusually subtle flavor. Cooked cauliflower, fried green pepper, sliced beets, French dressing, and a little tarragon seem to magically melt together to create a perfectly delicious salad. Serve at room temperature to enhance its mellow flavor.

INGREDIENTS
- 1 10-ounce package frozen cauliflower
- 1 green pepper
- 1 tablespoon butter
- 1 8-ounce can sliced beets
- 5 tablespoons French dressing
- 1/4 teaspoon tarragon

ASSEMBLE
- saucepan
- skillet
- paring knife
- set measuring spoons
- serving bowl
- salad fork and spoon
- salad plates

DIRECTIONS

Cook cauliflower according to directions on package. Meanwhile, discard seeds and pith from green pepper. Cut pepper pieces into slices and sauté in butter for one minute. Drain sliced beets and arrange in salad bowl. Drain cauliflower and arrange on beet slices. Arrange pepper slices nicely over all. Dribble dressing over salad, sprinkle with tarragon and serve at room temperature.

* May be prepared several hours before serving time. Keep at room temperature.

FRUIT AND CUCUMBER SALAD

Looking for a salad everyone will like? This combination of fresh fruit, cucumber, and French dressing is certain to please. It's so good that you can serve it as a main course at luncheon. Just arrange whole leaves of romaine lettuce on serving plates, top with this salad, and decorate with halves of peaches, pears, and cherries. Then prepare to sit back and take bows.

INGREDIENTS
2 fresh peaches
1 small or ½ large cucumber
4 halves canned pears
20 Bing cherries
¼ cup French dressing

ASSEMBLE
paring knife
large salad bowl
measuring cup
salad fork and spoon

DIRECTIONS
Peel and slice thinly peaches, pears and cucumbers. Arrange fruit in salad bowl. Cut 20 cherries in half, remove pits, and add cherry meats to salad bowl. Toss with French dressing. Serve immediately.

GARNISH *(Optional)*
Decorate center of salad by making a flower of cherry halves. Cut a "stem" of cucumber peel and put at one side of the cherry flower. Place a whole mint leaf on either side of the cucumber peel "stem." Serve immediately.

CAESAR SALAD

Truly the Caesar among salads! Don't let the fame of this salad frighten you away. This recipe works every time.

INGREDIENTS

1 cup packaged croutons or 2
  slices day-old bread
3 tablespoons olive oil
1/2 head romaine lettuce
2 cloves garlic
1 teaspoon salt
1 egg yolk
1/4 cup olive oil
1 tablespoon lemon juice
1/8 teaspoon pepper, coarsely
  ground
8 anchovy fillets (flat)
1/4 cup grated Parmesan cheese

ASSEMBLE

small skillet
measuring cup
set measuring spoons
spoon
paring knife
garlic press
paper towels
salad bowl
salad fork and spoon

DIRECTIONS

Fry croutons in 3 tablespoons olive oil for one minute. Stir often. Wash lettuce and drain on paper towels. Peel and crush garlic and place in salad bowl with salt. Mash garlic and salt together with back of spoon. Add egg yolk and mix well. Add olive oil, lemon juice, and pepper. Mix. Break lettuce into 2-inch pieces and toss with dressing in salad bowl. Drain anchovy fillets on paper towels. Cut into fourths. Sprinkle Parmesan cheese, anchovies, and croutons over salad. Serve immediately.

LEBANESE SALAD

Here is a salad that has everything: the "salady" flavor of tomato and romaine lettuce, the zest of scallions and mint, and the crunchiness of wheat germ.

INGREDIENTS

1/2 head romaine lettuce
1 large tomato
2 scallions, trimmed
20 fresh mint leaves; 1 tablespoon
   dried mint may be substituted
   if necessary
3 tablespoons olive oil
3 tablespoons vinegar (white
   wine is best)
2 tablespoons wheat germ
1/8 teaspoon salt
pepper to taste

ASSEMBLE

paring knife
salad bowl
set measuring spoons
paper towels
salad fork and spoon
salad plates

DIRECTIONS

Wash lettuce, drain on paper towels and break into one-inch pieces. Arrange in salad bowl. Chop scallions, tomato, and mint leaves. Arrange on lettuce in salad bowl. Sprinkle oil, vinegar and wheat germ, over salad. Add salt and pepper to taste. Serve cold.

ITALIAN WHITE BEAN AND ANCHOVY SALAD*

This white bean salad starts like the French one, with the smooth richness of white beans and olive oil. Then the dash and excitement of Italian cooking takes over to create a salad spiked with anchovies and black olives. It's really good!

INGREDIENTS

2 cups white beans, measured
   after rinsing heavy juice from
   beans in colander
10 black olives, pitted
4 anchovy fillets, flat
1 tablespoon capers
1/4 cup olive oil
1 clove garlic, peeled
1 tablespoon lemon juice
2 sprigs parsley
1/2 teaspoon basil leaves

ASSEMBLE

large mixing bowl
small mixing bowl
can opener
garlic press
paring knife
set measuring spoons
colander
measuring cup
paper towels
salad bowl
salad fork and spoon

DIRECTIONS

Measure beans into mixing bowl. Slice olives into circles. Drain anchovies on paper towels, then cut into quarters and add to mixing bowl along with olives and capers. Measure olive oil into small mixing bowl. Add crushed garlic and lemon juice and stir well. Pour over bean salad mixture and toss lightly. Place salad in salad bowl.

GARNISH

Wash and chop 2 sprigs of parsley. Sprinkle salad with chopped parsley and basil. Serve at room temperature.

* May be prepared 24 hours in advance. Refrigerate. Allow to come to room temperature before serving.

BEAN AND SAUSAGE SALAD

Have an extra-special salad to lunch! Try this savory combination of sausage slices, red and green peppers, kidney beans and chickpeas topped with hard-cooked eggs.

INGREDIENTS
6 cooked sausages
2½ tablespoons vegetable oil
2 cloves garlic, peeled
4 scallions, with 3 inches of
  green top
½ cup Your Own Freezer Red
  Peppers (see page 235)
½ cup Your Own Freezer Green
  Peppers (see page 235)
1 cup each canned red and white
  kidney beans
1 cup canned chickpeas
2 hard-cooked eggs, shelled and
  sliced
2 lettuce leaves
salt and pepper

ASSEMBLE
medium-sized skillet
sharp knife
set measuring spoons
colander
measuring cup
mixing spoon
2 serving plates

DIRECTIONS
Slice the sausages in ¼-inch rounds. Sauté in the oil for 2 minutes, stirring frequently. Meanwhile, mince the garlic and set it aside. Coarsely chop the scallions. Remove the sausage slices from the pan with a slotted spoon and keep them warm. Measure the beans and chickpeas into the colander and drain well.

Add the garlic, the red and green peppers, and the scallions to the oil in the skillet. Stir over medium heat for one minute. Add the drained beans and half the sausage slices and stir gently for one minute more. Arrange the lettuce leaves on serving plates, divide the bean salad between each, then top each salad with half the egg slices and remaining sausage slices. Serve immediately.

Start with a head of lettuce and take it from there. The following are recipes that can turn simple, fresh greens into salads par excellence with a mere flip of the wrist.

CREAMY BLUE CHEESE SALAD DRESSING

An extra-special blue cheese dressing that is smooth and unusually flavored with chervil, tarragon and nutmeg. Subtle, but pungent enough to give character to almost any combination of greens.

INGREDIENTS
5 tablespoons blue cheese
½ cup heavy cream
1 teaspoon tarragon
3 tablespoons lemon juice
½ teaspoon chervil
¼ teaspoon salt
⅛ teaspoon coarse black pepper
1 generous pinch nutmeg
½ clove garlic, peeled and
   crushed

ASSEMBLE
mixing bowl
set measuring spoons
measuring cup
spoon

DIRECTIONS
Mix blue cheese and heavy cream until smooth. Add the remaining ingredients and mix thoroughly. Serve cold.

GREEN GODDESS SALAD DRESSING*

Delicate green and serene is this blender-smooth dressing for salads. Make it in an instant and serve it on Bibb lettuce for a salad amiable enough to accompany any meal. Good with seafood, too.

INGREDIENTS

1/2 cup mayonnaise
1/4 cup sour cream
1 tablespoon tarragon vinegar
1 tablespoon lemon juice
1 tablespoon Your Own Freezer
  Onion (see page 237)
2 anchovy fillets
1 tablespoon chopped scallion
  tops
2 tablespoons Your Own Freezer
  Parsley (see page 240)
1 clove garlic, peeled and
  crushed
1/8 teaspoon black pepper

ASSEMBLE

measuring cup
set measuring spoons
blender
paring knife
spoon or rubber spatula

DIRECTIONS

Place all ingredients in electric blender container. Cover and blend at high speed for about 20 seconds. Stop blender and scrape down sides of container with spoon or spatula. Blend for 10 seconds more. Serve cold.

* May be prepared 24 hours in advance of serving. Refrigerate until needed.

ANTIPASTO SALAD DRESSING*

Here's a salad treat with the zip of vegetables right in the dressing. All you need is crisp lettuce to create a salad that's not only good to eat but colorful as well.

INGREDIENTS

2 slices salami
2 tablespoons Your Own Freezer
  Onion (see page 237)
1 tablespoon chopped green
  pepper
1 tablespoon chopped pimiento
1 tablespoon pitted and chopped
  black olives
½ cup olive oil
5 tablespoons red wine vinegar
⅛ teaspoon salt
2 garlic cloves, peeled and
  crushed

ASSEMBLE

small mixing bowl
set measuring spoons
measuring cup
garlic press
paring knife

DIRECTIONS

Slice salami into very fine strips about one inch long. Place all chopped vegetables in mixing bowl with olive oil, wine vinegar, salt, and garlic cloves. Add salami and stir vigorously. Serve cold.

* May be prepared 24 hours in advance of serving. Refrigerate until needed.

Vegetables

Silent partners of the meal

Hors d'oeuvres are beautiful promises; soups are liquid gold; salads are pace-changers; entrées are promises come true. Is there nothing in a meal that is unimportant? No, but there are some things that are less important than others, and vegetables fall into that category. The more carefully they are chosen, the less important they become. Then why pick them carefully? Simply because vegetables are performing their function perfectly if they blend smoothly and unobtrusively with the rest of the meal. Of course they should be perfectly prepared, colorful and wonderfully tasty, but equally important, they should be minor planets totally eclipsed by their entrée.

To determine whether the vegetables you have chosen are right for the meal they are to accompany, taste the main course and the vegetables together to see if they blend. They can differ, but they must blend well. After a little practice, you will be able to do your tasting mentally and avoid a lot of trouble. Just "think" the tastes of your entrée and vegetables, one after the other, and if one seems to jar your "mental" taste buds it is likely something should be changed. To see if your mental tester is operating properly, "think" two foods that do not seem to go well together, such as shrimp and garlic butter with sugar and heavy cream. Ugh. Now "think" two foods that go marvelously together such as prosciutto and melon. Yum. Every time you prepare a meal try this test before you actually taste anything. Before long you'll be able to pick up a cookbook and "taste" your way into seventh heaven.

After you have taste-tested the vegetables you have chosen to accompany your dinner, test them for eye appeal. Visualize them on the dishes from which they are to be eaten. White against white? Fine—if they are dressed up with pieces of black truffle, a touch of paprika, a border of parsley. But if everything in the meal is light or white, shouldn't you use a vegetable with a similar taste but a different color?

And what about texture? Before you choose a creamed vegetable, go over your menu and be sure you haven't inadvertently chosen a creamy hors d'oeuvre, a cream soup, a salad with a creamy dressing, an entrée in a rich, creamy sauce and . . . I'm sure you haven't, but the tastes do go well together and it is easy to get so excited over an individual dish that you don't realize until too late that the foods you've chosen are too similar.

Summing up then, choose vegetables carefully to round out the meal but to be completely subordinate to the entrée. They should be secondary but never drab, silently impressive, always backing the main course with a show of quiet strength.

GREEN ONIONS WITH LEMON-CLAM SAUCE

Tender cooked green onions with a lovely lemony clam sauce.
Perfect with almost any meal.

INGREDIENTS
1 cup hot water
12 young green onions or scal-
    lions, about the thickness of
    a pencil*
6 tablespoons butter
1 tablespoon lemon juice
4 tablespoons minced clams

ASSEMBLE
cooking pan with 8-inch
    bottom
skillet
set measuring spoons
tablespoon
paper towels
2 individual serving plates

DIRECTIONS
Place hot water and washed, trimmed scallions in cooking pan.
Cook over high flame for 4 minutes. Meanwhile melt butter in
skillet. Add lemon juice and minced clams. Heat. Drain scallions and place on paper towels. Place hot scallions, 6 each, on
the two plates. Reheat clam sauce if not hot. Divide sauce
evenly on the two mounds of scallions. Serve hot.

NOTE
* When trimming scallions leave 4 inches of green top.

GARLIC CHERRY TOMATOES
(serves 4)

Round, red bits of goodness—cherry tomatoes all warm and buttery and flavored with garlic. Marvelous as a vegetable, attractive as a garnish and capable of functioning as both at once!

INGREDIENTS
1 pint box cherry tomatoes
¼ pound butter
1 clove garlic, peeled and
   crushed
salt and black pepper

ASSEMBLE
skillet
set measuring spoons
tablespoon
serving dish

DIRECTIONS
Place skillet over low heat. Add butter and melt. Add garlic to butter. Heat but do not brown. Add tomatoes. Heat for 4 minutes over very low flame. Sprinkle with salt and pepper to taste. Serve immediately.

GARNISH *(Optional)*
Place tomatoes on a bed of watercress. Tuck sprigs of watercress among tomatoes. Serve hot.

FLUFFY CORN FRITTERS

Light-as-a-feather corn fritters, fantastic when topped with maple syrup or simply delicious when served on their own.

INGREDIENTS
6 young ears fresh corn
4 egg whites
¼ cup vegetable oil
salt

ASSEMBLE
skillet
grater
table knife
eggbeater
2 mixing bowls
measuring cup

DIRECTIONS
Rub the corn kernels against the grater to remove as much corn as is possible. Scrape the cob with a table knife to remove any remaining juice. In another bowl beat the egg whites until stiff. Pour the oil into the skillet and heat to moderate-high. Gently fold the beaten egg whites into the grated corn. Do not stir or mix too briskly. Spoon the corn and egg white mixture a tablespoonful at a time into the hot oil. Fry until golden and then turn gently and fry until done. Sprinkle with salt. Serve immediately while very hot.

CARROTS AND WHITE GRAPES

A colorful and tasty vegetable dish. You'll be surprised how well grapes behave as a vegetable.

INGREDIENTS
1 13½-ounce can small whole
   Belgian carrots
30 seedless white grapes
4 tablespoons butter
4 tablespoons Cointreau
   (optional)

ASSEMBLE
skillet
set measuring spoons
paper towels
tablespoon
serving bowl

DIRECTIONS
Drain carrots and blot dry on paper towels. Wash grapes and dry in similar manner. Melt butter over medium flame. Add Cointreau. Stir. Add grapes and carrots and cook over low flame for 4 minutes. Stir frequently. Serve hot.

NOTE
To serve 3, add 20 grapes. To serve 4, double recipe.

GARNISH
Tuck pairs of fresh mint leaves here and there among grapes and carrots. Serve hot.

FRIED GREEN PEPPERS*

Onions do their bit, and so does French dressing, but the green peppers are really the star of the show.

INGREDIENTS
1 tablespoon olive oil
1 tablespoon butter
3 green peppers, cut into one-inch
  strips
2 small onions, peeled and
  cut into rings
2 tablespoons French dressing
pinch dry mustard

ASSEMBLE
skillet
paring knife
set measuring spoons
paper towels
serving dish

DIRECTIONS
Place olive oil and butter in skillet. Add green pepper strips and onion slices to skillet. Fry over medium flame until onions just begin to brown. Remove from heat and add French dressing and dry mustard. Stir until mixed. Serve immediately.

* May be prepared an hour before serving. Fry peppers and onions for 2 minutes only and remove from flame. Five minutes before serving time, continue frying for 3 or 4 minutes more. Add French dressing and mustard and serve hot.

VEGETABLES IN CREAM

If you're tired of the same old mixed vegetables, keep this recipe in mind. The real surprise is the lettuce, a vegetable often cooked in France but seldom in America.

INGREDIENTS	ASSEMBLE
½ 10-ounce package frozen peas and carrots	saucepan
	set measuring spoons
½ head lettuce	skillet with cover
8 scallions	colander
4 tablespoons butter	spoon
¼ teaspoon sugar	paring knife
2 tablespoons water	paper towels
4 tablespoons heavy cream	serving dish

DIRECTIONS

Cook peas and carrots according to directions on package. Meanwhile, wash the lettuce and drain it on paper towels. Wash scallions and cut off roots. Cut 4 scallions into pieces ½ inch long, including several inches of the green top. Slice lettuce into strips ½ inch wide and 3 inches long. Melt butter in skillet. Add sugar, lettuce, chopped scallions plus 4 whole scallions, and two tablespoons water. Cover and steam cook over medium heat for 3 minutes. If skillet should cook dry, add 2 more tablespoons water. Add heavy cream. Cook without boiling for one minute. Drain peas and carrots. Mound peas, carrots, and chopped scallions in center of serving dish. Place cooked lettuce on one side of serving dish and cooked whole scallions on the other side. Serve hot.

NOTE

To serve 3, use entire package of peas and carrots and one additional scallion. To serve 4, double entire recipe.

GARNISH *(Optional)*

Crisscross scallions with strips of pimiento. Sprinkle peas, carrots, and chopped scallions with one tablespoon hard-cooked egg yolk pushed through a sieve. Place a slice hard-cooked egg on lettuce strips. Top with a caper. Serve hot.

CAULIFLOWER WITH ALMONDS

A marvelous combination of tastes. Crispy almonds and golden crumbs crown snowy flowerets of cauliflower and garlic.

INGREDIENTS
1 10-ounce package frozen
   cauliflower
¼ cup butter
½ cup bread crumbs
¾ cup slivered almonds
1 clove garlic, peeled and
   minced
1 teaspoon salt

ASSEMBLE
saucepan
skillet
spoon
serving dish

DIRECTIONS

Cook cauliflower according to directions on package. Sauté butter, crumbs, almonds, and garlic in skillet until almonds and crumbs are golden in color. Pour over cauliflower. Serve hot.

GARNISH *(Optional)*
Tuck small pieces of parsley among the cauliflower flowerets and sprinkle with paprika. Serve hot.

GREEN BEANS AND ONIONS AU BEURRE*

A marvelous, subtle accompaniment.

INGREDIENTS
½ 9-ounce package frozen green
    beans (cut green beans,
    Italian green beans,
    Frenched green beans all
    equally delicious prepared
    this way)
½ teaspoon salt
4 tablespoons butter
2 small onions
1 tablespoon wine vinegar

ASSEMBLE
medium-sized saucepan
medium-sized skillet
set measuring spoons
paring knife
spoon
serving dish

DIRECTIONS
Cook beans according to directions on package. Meanwhile, melt butter in skillet. Peel the onions, slice into thin slices and add to skillet. Cook. Drain cooked beans. Add to skillet. Cook until both beans and onions begin to brown. Add vinegar, stir, and serve hot.

NOTE
To serve 3, double quantity of frozen string beans. To serve 4, double entire recipe.

* May be prepared in advance and reheated at serving time.

GREEN BEANS SERBIAN*

This is really something special! Drained green beans mixed with crumbs sautéed golden brown in butter, finely minced parsley stirred in, and the whole casserole topped with sour cream and baked.

INGREDIENTS

1 9-ounce package frozen green
   beans
salt according to directions on
   package
⅓ cup sweet butter
2 tablespoons bread crumbs
¼ cup Your Own Freezer
   Parsley (see page 240)
1 clove garlic, peeled and
   crushed
¼ teaspoon freshly ground
   black pepper
¾ cup sour cream

ASSEMBLE

saucepan
skillet
measuring cup
colander
set measuring spoons
paring knife
tablespoon
flameproof dish or casserole

DIRECTIONS

Set oven at 450°. Cook green beans in the saucepan according to directions on package. Meanwhile, place skillet over medium-high heat. Add butter. When melted add bread crumbs. Stir until lightly browned. Remove from flame. Drain the green beans in colander. Put green beans, parsley, bread-crumb mixture, garlic, and pepper in baking dish. Stir.* Spread sour cream over bean mixture. Bake for 2 minutes. Serve immediately.

GARNISH *(Optional)*

Cut lemon to form a cup topped with points. Scoop out pulp. Fill with a large dollop of sour cream. Place in center of sour cream-covered beans. Arrange small strips of pimiento and lemon rind and 4 pieces of green bean in a design radiating out from the lemon cup. Sprinkle a border of finely chopped parsley around the edge of the sour cream. Place a pinch of paprika at 2-inch intervals around sour cream, close to the parsley border. Bake 2 minutes, as above. Serve hot. Sprinkle chopped parsley around sour cream in lemon cup. Dot center of cup with pimiento squares.

* May be prepared several hours in advance of serving. Bring recipe to this point. Heat beans in oven 10 minutes prior to serving.

NEW PEAS WITH MINT

Do you need an unobtrusive vegetable to round out the meal you have planned? Here, tender new peas get together with butter, oregano, and just enough mint. A quiet spot with a lot of flavor.

INGREDIENTS

1 10-ounce package frozen new
  or baby peas
2 tablespoons butter
½ cup fresh mint leaves,
  chopped; 1½ tablespoons dried
  mint leaves may be
  substituted if necessary
¼ teaspoon salt
¼ teaspoon oregano

ASSEMBLE

saucepan
measuring cup
colander
paring knife
serving dish

DIRECTIONS

Cook peas according to directions on package. Drain well. Melt butter in saucepan over medium heat. Add peas, chopped mint leaves, salt and oregano. Toss. Serve hot.

NOTE
Serves 2 or 3.

GARNISH

Tuck whole mint leaves here and there among the peas. Serve hot.

ARTICHOKES WITH FOIE GRAS

This is a marvelous vegetable to serve with any meal that needs a little dressing up. The rich, smooth combination of flavors seems to say, "This is a special meal for special people."

INGREDIENTS

4 artichoke bottoms (canned)
4 slices of foie gras
32 drops lemon juice
2 tablespoons butter
1 tablespoon flour
1/4 teaspoon salt
1 cup heavy cream
7 tablespoons packaged grated
  Swiss or Cheddar cheese

ASSEMBLE

can opener
sharp knife
set measuring spoons
measuring cup
medium-sized skillet
spoon
flameproof serving dish

DIRECTIONS

Turn broiler on high heat. Sprinkle each artichoke base with 8 drops of lemon juice and top each with a slice of foie gras. Melt butter in skillet, add flour and salt and stir until smooth. Pour in heavy cream and 4 tablespoons grated cheese. Stir over medium heat until fairly thick. Place pâté-topped artichoke bottoms in flameproof dish. Pour sauce over all. Sprinkle with 3 tablespoons grated cheese. Place under broiler until top begins to brown.

Go withs

"Little extras" that make the difference

Often in a really fine restaurant you will find "little extras" used to enhance the flavor or the appearance of the more important or substantial portions of the meal. Like a butterfly perched on a flower, the "go with" calls attention to the dish it accompanies without detracting in the least from its own beauty.

These eye- and palate-pleasing garnishes can make the difference between a really good meal that somehow fails to excite and a superb meal that is long remembered.

Serving Boeuf au Vin? Marvelous! Your friends will love it, but as delicious as it is, it will never be as exciting-looking as a fancy shrimp curry. But you can decorate the serving plate liberally with anchovies in cherry tomatoes, tuck sprigs of parsley around the edge to make an impression.

Treating your guests to Breast of Chicken in Rum Crumbs? Top with Marrons in Apricot Halves to dazzle your guests.

Use garnishes whenever you get the chance and you will have really memorable meals.

MARRONS AND APRICOTS

Here is a handsome garnish that has even more flavor than eye-appeal. The mellow goodness of marrons combines with honey-brushed apricots for a "go with" par excellence.

INGREDIENTS
2 fresh apricots
1 tablespoon honey
1 tablespoon butter
4 marrons glacés, available
   bottled in syrup

ASSEMBLE
paring knife
pastry brush
small baking dish

DIRECTIONS
Set broiler at high heat. Wash and dry apricots. Cut in half and remove pits. Brush apricot halves with honey. Place in buttered baking dish. Broil for one minute. Remove from broiler. Top each apricot half with one marron. Replace dish in broiler for one more minute. Serve hot or cold. Perfect garnish for chicken, duck, turkey, game birds or ham.

FRIED BANANAS

A garnish even more tempting to the palate than to the eye are these golden little rolls of fried banana. Serve hot with chicken, ham, curry, or any exotic meal for that something special.

INGREDIENTS
2 firm bananas
3 tablespoons light rum
1 egg
¼ cup vegetable oil
¼ cup bread crumbs

ASSEMBLE
paring knife
small bowl
fork
2 plates
skillet
measuring cup
paper towels

DIRECTIONS
Peel and slice bananas into one-inch pieces. Sprinkle with rum. Meanwhile beat egg in small bowl and put vegetable oil in skillet. Place skillet over high heat. Dip banana pieces in egg and then roll in bread crumbs. Drop into hot oil and fry until golden brown. Serve hot.

GRILLED CHEESE TOMATOES

These luscious cheese-topped grilled tomatoes provide an eye-filling, taste-tempting garnish to most meals. Particularly good with steak or any plain meat dish.

INGREDIENTS

2 tomatoes
2 tablespoons Your Own Freezer
  Shallots (see page 238)
garlic clove crushed
4 tablespoons butter
3 tablespoons fine bread crumbs
1 tablespoon grated Parmesan
  cheese
⅛ teaspoon salt
2 tablespoons grated Swiss cheese

ASSEMBLE

shallow baking dish
set measuring spoons
paring knife
skillet
spoon

DIRECTIONS

Turn broiler on high heat. Wash tomatoes. Cut in half and shake out the seeds. Grease baking dish and place tomato halves on it. Dot tomatoes with butter. Place under broiler. Meanwhile, sauté shallots and garlic in butter in skillet for one minute. Add bread crumbs, grated Parmesan cheese, and the salt. Stir. Remove baking dish from boiler. Divide the cheese-bread crumb mixture evenly over the four tomato halves. Top each with ½ tablespoon grated Swiss cheese. Replace under broiler for one minute. Serve very hot.

ANCHOVIES IN CHERRY TOMATOES*

A tiny but toothsome garnish that's equally tasty served hot or cold. Arrange them like little roses with watercress for leaves and they'll dress up any dish.

INGREDIENTS

10 cherry tomatoes
5 teaspoons fine bread crumbs
½ clove garlic, peeled and
    crushed
2 teaspoons anchovy oil
1 level teaspoon drained capers
10 rolled anchovy fillets

ASSEMBLE

small bowl
paring knife
very small spoon
set measuring spoons

DIRECTIONS

Slice ¼ inch off the top of each cherry tomato. With small spoon scoop out tomato pulp. In small bowl combine bread crumbs, the garlic, anchovy oil, and drained capers. Stir until well mixed. Fill each cherry tomato half-full of bread-crumb mixture. Top with rolled anchovy fillet. Anchovy should protrude from top of tomato. Use as garnish for any salad, steak or Tartar sandwiches. Serve hot or cold.

* These can be prepared up to 2 hours in advance of serving. To heat, place under broiler for a minute or two.

FANCY CHEESE CROUTONS FOR SOUP

This large, garlic-flavored, cheese-topped crouton is just the thing to turn any hot soup into a gourmet treat.

INGREDIENTS
2 tablespoons butter
½ clove garlic, peeled and crushed
2 slices French bread ½ inch thick; bread slices should not be too large
2 tablespoons grated Swiss cheese
10 small strips pimiento
2 rolled anchovies
12 capers

ASSEMBLE
bread knife
set measuring spoons
medium-sized skillet
paper towels

DIRECTIONS
Turn broiler on high heat. Place butter and garlic in skillet. Sauté the French bread in the butter until beginning to brown. Remove slices and place on paper towels. Sprinkle each slice thickly with grated Swiss cheese.

Drain 10 small pimiento strips and 2 anchovies on paper towel. Place a rolled anchovy fillet in the center of each slice of cheese-topped bread. Arrange the pimiento strips around the anchovy fillet, radiating outward. Place 3 capers on either side of the pimiento strips. Place under broiler until cheese begins to brown.

PETITE PEAS IN ARTICHOKE BOTTOMS

Here's a garnish that doubles as a vegetable: a superior combination of vegetables in a sophisticated sauce.

INGREDIENTS
½ can or package petite peas
4 artichoke bottoms, canned
  (12-ounce can)
2 tablespoons Your Own Freezer
  Shallots (see page 238)
3 tablespoons butter
10 drops vinegar (white wine)
¼ cup red wine
1 small bay leaf
1 pinch marjoram
1 pinch thyme
1 teaspoon parsley flakes
1 pinch black pepper
⅓ teaspoon salt
¼ cup canned consommé
  (undiluted)
10 drops lemon juice

ASSEMBLE
small saucepan
can opener
paring knife
measuring cup
set measuring spoons
tablespoon
small skillet
small strainer
sauceboat

DIRECTIONS
Cook peas in a small saucepan. Drain artichoke bottoms and place in skillet. Place shallots, one tablespoon butter, and vinegar in skillet. Heat for one minute. Remove artichokes. Place in serving dish. Add wine, bay leaf, marjoram. thyme, parsley flakes, pepper, and salt to skillet, boil for one minute. Add consommé. Boil for 2 minutes longer. Strain sauce into cup. Return to skillet. Stir in lemon juice and remaining butter.

Drain peas. Add peas and artichoke bottoms to sauce for one minute. Remove artichoke bottoms from pan. Place on serving dish. Mound peas on artichoke bottoms. Serve remaining sauce separately. Serve hot.

GARNISH *(Optional)*

Place large slice cooked carrot on each mound of peas. Top carrot slice with one small slice black truffle, a tiny amount sieved hard-cooked egg yolk, and one caper. Serve immediately.

FLAMED SPICED PEACHES

If you love the effect of foods served flambé but think it's too difficult to be practical, this easy-to-prepare garnish may change your mind. Flame these peaches with brandy and serve with any poultry or game bird, or alone as a dessert.

INGREDIENTS

4 Your Own Freezer Peach
   Halves (see page 245) or
   canned freestone peach halves or
   whole spiced peaches
3 whole cloves for every peach
   half
¼ cup brandy
¼ cup honey
⅛ teaspoon nutmeg

ASSEMBLE

chafing dish
Sterno
can opener
measuring cup
ladle

DIRECTIONS

Drain canned peaches. Decorate each peach half or spiced peach with 3 cloves. Arrange peaches, flat side down, in blazer pan of chafing dish. Heat for one minute over low flame. Add most of brandy to peaches. Pour the rest into the ladle. Heat by holding a match under one ladle. When brandy is warm, light with a match. Pour the flaming brandy over the peaches and brandy in the chafing dish. When flame goes out stir in honey and the nutmeg. Allow to bubble for a minute. Serve hot.

CURRIED PINEAPPLE SLICES

A marvelous accompaniment to a wide variety of meals. You'll love it served with game, fowl, or any meal inspired by the islands. Also delicious with curry.

INGREDIENTS
2 tablespoons butter
4 tablespoons pineapple liquid
2 tablespoons sugar
1 tablespoon rum
¼ teaspoon curry powder
4 slices canned pineapple
12 maraschino cherries

ASSEMBLE
medium-sized skillet
can opener
spoon
set measuring spoons

DIRECTIONS
Melt butter over medium heat. Add pineapple liquid, sugar, rum, and curry powder. Stir over high heat for one minute. Add pineapple slices and cherries. Cook over high heat for 2 minutes. Serve hot or cold.

HAM CORNUCOPIAS

*Roll up a few of these cornucopias the next time you're serving
a cold salad or cold buffet. You'll find them a tasty, handy, and
decorative trim for nearly any simple meal.*

INGREDIENTS
1 3-ounce package cream cheese
1 tablespoon heavy cream
2 tablespoons crabmeat, chopped
2 tablespoons finely chopped
  celery
½ cup finely chopped pistachio
  or walnut meats
4 large, thin slices of cold boiled,
  ham, available at any delicatessen

ASSEMBLE
small mixing bowl
fork
teaspoon
paring knife

DIRECTIONS
Place cream cheese in mixing bowl along with heavy cream.
Mix until creamy. Add crabmeat, celery and ¼ cup nut meats.
Mix. Lay each ham slice out flat. Spoon 3 tablespoons cream
cheese nut mixture on each. Roll ham slices into cornucopias.
Allow some of cheese mixture to protrude from the open ends.
Dip cheese end in remaining chopped nuts. Serve cold.

GLAZED APPLE RINGS

Decorate roast pork, roast chicken, pork chops, or ham with these spicy red glazed apple rings for a touch of color and a ton of taste. As a garnish at Christmas, color some green. Even Saint Nick will stay for dinner.

INGREDIENTS
3 medium-sized apples
1 teaspoon plus 6 drops red food
  coloring
1 tablespoon water
3 tablespoons butter
¼ cup brown sugar
½ teaspoon nutmeg
½ teaspoon cinnamon
¼ teaspoon ground cloves

ASSEMBLE
shallow baking dish
cup (for food coloring)
apple corer
paring knife
set measuring spoons
small bowl
measuring cup

DIRECTIONS

Set broiler on high flame. Peel and core apples. Slice into rings ½ inch thick. Mix one teaspoon red food coloring with one tablespoon water. Dip apple slices in food coloring, pat dry. Dot bottom of baking dish with butter. Place apple rings in baking dish. Mix sugar with 6 drops food coloring. Sprinkle apple slices with the sugar and spices and place under broiler until sugar becomes glazed. Serve hot.

Desserts

The sirens of the dinner

With all the care and concern lavished on the rest of the meal, no matter how important or imposing the entrée, it is generally the dessert that is the siren of the dinner.

This final course not only holds its own among the other delectable elements of the meal, but generally steals hearts with outrageous lack of concern for the dignity of the main course.

But for all its scene stealing, the dessert must not be singled out for this reason alone. It is most important that the dessert complement the entire meal. First choose the main course, then the first course, soup, vegetables and salad and finally a dessert.

Select a light syrupy or fruity dessert such as Pêches Flambées for a meal that tends to be slightly heavy. Decide upon a rich, creamy trifle as a close for a moderately plain meal. Or flame up a chafing dish of perfection, Crêpes Suzette, as an exciting climax to that meal of many minor climaxes, the French dinner.

Bewitching though the variety of desserts may be, all have one function: to end the meal perfectly.

CHAMPAGNE FRUIT COCKTAIL

A ladylike dessert? Perhaps, but one that may mellow the lady considerably. On the other hand, her companion may be too involved with dessert to notice. If he is, more's the pity. A terrible waste to serve to more than the two of you.

INGREDIENTS

4 Your Own Freezer Peach
   Halves (see page 245) or
   canned peach halves
10 large fresh strawberries, hulled
4 sugar cubes soaked with bitters
1 bottle iced champagne

ASSEMBLE

can opener
corkscrew
2 champagne glasses
serving plate
serving spoon

DIRECTIONS

Defrost freezer peaches or drain 4 canned halves. Arrange fruit on serving plate. Top each peach half with one cube of sugar soaked with bitters (Be careful not to dissolve sugar cubes with bitters. Just dampen them.) Open champagne at table and place one peach half with sugar cube and several strawberries in each champagne glass. Pour champagne over fruit. The fruit-champagne ratio depends on the diner's addiction to either fruit or champagne.

PÊCHES FLAMBÉES

Fresh, ripe peaches, poached in syrup, set like a golden crown on a mound of macaroon crumbs, and finally, flamed with Cointreau. A perfect dessert. Not too heavy, but rich enough to satisfy the most avid dessert eater.

INGREDIENTS

2 fully ripe fresh peaches, or 4
   Your Own Freezer Peach
   Halves (see page 245)
1 cup boiling water
¾ cup boiling water
¾ cup sugar
10 drops lemon juice
8 tablespoons macaroon crumbs
   or 4 macaroons
4 tablespoons Cointreau (rum
   may be substituted)

ASSEMBLE

Pyrex bowl
paring knife
small saucepan
set measuring spoons
box matches
chafing dish (2 quart size)
serving spoon
2 serving plates

DIRECTIONS

Place fresh peaches in Pyrex bowl. Pour one cup boiling water over them. Lift out each peach, cut in half, and gently remove the pit. Gently pull off the skin with paring knife. (If you are using freezer peach halves, begin recipe here.) Place ¾ cup boiling water and sugar in saucepan. Place over high flame. Add peach halves and 10 drops lemon juice to syrup in pan. Boil for 2 minutes. Meanwhile make 2 mounds of 2 tablespoons macaroon crumbs each on each serving plate. Place peaches and syrup in blazer pan of chafing dish. Arrange serving plates with macaroon crumbs on tray. When ready to serve, carry chafing dish and serving plates to table. Heat peaches and syrup over medium flame. Pour Cointreau gently over peaches in syrup. Do not stir. Light Cointreau with a match. This will be easy after the Cointreau is heated slightly by the hot syrup. Place a peach half on each mound of crumbs. Spoon 6 tablespoons of Cointreau-syrup mixture over each peach half. Serve immediately.

APPLE COINTREAU SUNDAE

If this sounds too easy to be good, you have a pleasant surprise in store. Fresh, crispy apple slices combined with ice cream would be a treat even without the satiny smooth taste of the Cointreau, but with it . . . well, taste it and see!

INGREDIENTS

1 fresh apple
2 scoops vanilla ice cream
2 tablespoons Cointreau

ASSEMBLE

ice cream scoop
paring knife
silver dishes

DIRECTIONS

Peel the apple and cut into thin, unbroken slices. Arrange neatly around edge of the dishes. Scoop out large scoop of ice cream and place in the middle of the apple slices. Add Cointreau. Serve immediately.

GARNISH

Place 2 slices of apple in center of ice cream. Place whole blanched almond on either side. Serve immediately.

HOT CHERRY SUNDAE

If you like cherries you'll love this! Spicy cherries and cherry liqueur served hot over ice cream. Easy to make.

INGREDIENTS
½ 1-pound can black or tart cherries
½ teaspoon cornstarch
1 or 2 sticks cinnamon
6 whole cloves or ¼ teaspoon ground cloves
1 teaspoon frozen orange juice concentrate
¼ cup Cherry Heering or similar sweet liqueur
2 large scoops vanilla ice cream

ASSEMBLE
large pan
can opener
tablespoon
set measuring spoons
measuring cup
silver dishes

DIRECTIONS
Stir cherries, cornstarch, cinnamon, cloves, and orange juice into a pan. Add the Cherry Heering and bring to a boil, stirring constantly. Scoop the ice cream into individual dishes and top with the hot cherries. Serve immediately. This can be made in a chafing dish.

STRAWBERRY TRIFLE*
(serves 2-3)

A dessert the English hold dear . . . and little wonder! This mellow blending of strawberries, cake, and vanilla cream couldn't be more delicious.

INGREDIENTS

2 cups light cream
1 3½-ounce package instant vanilla pudding
1 package ladyfingers
4 tablespoons sherry
20 fresh whole strawberries
1 10-ounce package frozen strawberries in syrup, defrosted
whipped cream

ASSEMBLE

mixing bowl
egg beater
set measuring spoons
measuring cup
paring knife
spoon
glass serving dish

DIRECTIONS

Place light cream in mixing bowl. Add instant vanilla pudding. Beat with eggbeater until pudding begins to thicken. Line sides and bottom of serving dish with ½ thickness of ladyfingers. Sprinkle with 2 tablespoons sherry. Cut 10 strawberries into thin slices. Spoon a layer of frozen strawberries and syrup onto lady fingers in bottom of dish. Cover with fresh strawberry slices. Spread a layer of instant pudding over strawberries and continue to fill serving dish with alternate layers of ladyfingers (sprinkled with sherry), strawberries in syrup, fresh strawberries, and pudding until dish is filled. End with layer of pudding.*

GARNISH

Cut 9 strawberries into quarters. Place remaining whole strawberry in center of trifle. Decorate top of serving dish neatly
with remaining pieces of strawberry. Pipe small points of
whipped cream around strawberry. Serve immediately.

* May be prepared 24 hours in advance. Refrigerate until needed. Garnish at last moment.

GREEK PONTICA

Yummy little fried cakes, as warm and golden as the Greek sun, served crispy and tempting under a blanket of honey and pistachio nuts.

INGREDIENTS
4 slices white bread
1 package shelled pistachio nuts
6 tablespoons honey
1 egg
1 tablespoon milk
½ cup bread crumbs
5 tablespoons butter

ASSEMBLE
chafing dish
round cookie cutter (or glass)
shallow bowl for beaten egg
2 small bowls for honey and nuts
plate for fried bread rounds
set measuring spoons
large skillet
measuring cup
rolling pin
serving plates
Sterno

DIRECTIONS
Cut bread into rounds using cookie cutter. Crush shelled nuts with rolling pin. Place in small bowl. Measure honey into small bowl. Beat egg and milk in shallow bowl. Measure bread crumbs into plate. Measure one tablespoon butter into blazer pan. Place chafing dish and dishes containing nuts and honey on a tray ready for cooking at table. Meanwhile dip bread rounds quickly in egg and then in bread crumbs, and fry them in skillet containing the remaining butter. If not using chafing dish, simply spoon one tablespoon honey and nuts over bread rounds and serve. Otherwise place fried bread rounds on tray until serving time. When ready to serve dessert, carry tray and chafing dish to table. Light Sterno under blazer pan and warm fried bread rounds in the melted butter. Place bread rounds on plates, cover each with a tablespoon of honey and sprinkle with chopped pistachio nuts. Serve immediately.

NOTE
More honey may be used if desired.

APPLE PANCAKE

This is a dish you will whip up not only for dessert but also for lunch, for Sunday brunch and on the spur of the moment for your late-hour guests.

INGREDIENTS

¼ cup all-purpose flour
3 tablespoons sugar
1 egg, beaten
½ cup light cream
2 teaspoons melted butter or
    vegetable oil
2 tablespoons butter
1 apple, peeled and thinly sliced
¼ teaspoon cinnamon
1 teaspoon lime juice

ASSEMBLE

mixing bowl
2 measuring cups
set measuring spoons
fork
paring knife
10-inch flameproof skillet
pancake turner
serving plates

DIRECTIONS

Set oven at broil. Mix flour and 2 tablespoons sugar. Beat together egg, cream, and melted shortening. Add liquid mixture to dry ingredients. Mix well. Melt one tablespoon butter in skillet. Pour in all of the pancake batter. Cook until golden brown over medium heat. Do not turn.

Meanwhile, peel and slice apple into ¼-inch slices. Arrange apple on uncooked top of pancake. Sprinkle with one tablespoon sugar and the cinnamon. Dot with remainder of butter. Cook for 2 minutes under broiler, taking care not to burn. Remove from flame and fold carefully with pancake turner. Sprinkle with a few grains of sugar and the lime juice. Cut in half and serve immediately.

SHERBET IN ORANGE CUPS

A beautiful way to serve sherbet. The orange itself becomes the serving dish. More than a dessert—a conversation piece.

INGREDIENTS

2 large thick-skinned oranges

2 small scoops pineapple sherbet. If not available, use lemon sherbet.

2 large scoops orange sherbet

4 fresh mint leaves

2 kumquats

ASSEMBLE

large ice cream scoop

small ice-cream scoop

paring knife

DIRECTIONS

Cut through the rind only around the middle (equator) of one orange. Be careful not to cut into the orange itself. Gently loosen skin with tip of knife. Carefully pull half of the rind up to form a cup at the top of the orange. This cup should still be attached to the orange itself. Now carefully pull down the other half of the orange rind to form another cup at the bottom of the orange. This, too, should remain attached to the orange. Repeat process with other orange.

Pull off any strings of white pith that may be on the cup or orange. Stand the oranges upright so that one of the orange skins forms a cup. In the open orange skin cup put a large scoop of orange sherbet. Top this with a small scoop of pineapple sherbet. Place a kumquat on top of this with a mint leaf on either side. Serve immediately.

CRÊPES SUZETTE*

Traditional. French. Delicious. A dessert that deserves its fame. Thin little pancakes with orange-brandy sauce, deliciously simple and vice versa.

INGREDIENTS

1 egg
½ cup milk
½ cup sifted flour
¼ teaspoon salt
NOTE: 1 can plain crêpes may be
  substituted for the above if
  desired
2 tablespoons butter
¼ cup butter
4 teaspoons confectioners sugar
1 orange
¼ cup Cointreau
¼ cup brandy

ASSEMBLE

mixing bowl
egg beater
grater
2 tablespoons
set measuring spoons
measuring cup
griddle or skillet
chafing dish or skillet
box matches
serving plates

DIRECTIONS

In the mixing bowl beat the egg with eggbeater. Add ½-cup milk, the flour, and salt and quickly beat with beater until batter is smooth.*

Grease griddle with a bit of butter and bake 6 three-inch pancakes or crêpes over medium-high flame. (Use 2 tablespoons batter for each crêpe and rotate the skillet rapidly after each addition to spread the batter evenly over the surface of the pan.) Fold the crêpes in half and then in half again. Turn off the flame under griddle but leave crêpes on griddle to keep warm. Melt ¼ cup butter in blazer pan of a chafing dish or

skillet. When butter begins to bubble, add the folded crêpes and sprinkle each with a teaspoonful of the powdered sugar. Cut orange in half. When the crêpes are hot, squeeze the orange juice into the pan. Add the Cointreau to the juice and spoon this sauce over the crêpes until they are thoroughly soaked through. Pour brandy over the top of the crêpes on each serving plate. Spoon a little of the remaining sauce over each crêpe. Serve immediately.

* If possible, set the batter aside for 2 hours before preparing crêpes.

COLD GERMAN FRUIT SOUP IN CANTALOUPE SHELLS*

Try this one for a cool and filling start or finish to a light meal or lunch. Zesty orange and cherry flavors in a spice-spiked soup. And you can eat the bowl.

INGREDIENTS
- 1 cantaloupe
- 1 1-pound can cold (thickened) cherry pie filling
- 1 teaspoon cinnamon
- 1 generous pinch powdered cloves
- ½ cup cold orange juice
- 2 whole sticks cinnamon
- 1 can instant whipped cream

ASSEMBLE
- blender
- measuring cup
- paring knife
- spoon
- can opener

DIRECTIONS

Pare the rind carefully from one whole cantaloupe. Slice the melon neatly in half. Remove pulp, seeds, and enough melon from center to hold soup. Place cherry pie filling, cinnamon, cloves, and orange juice in blender. Blend on high speed for one minute or until smooth. Pour cherry-orange mixture into cantaloupe shells. Decorate each with stick cinnamon.

GARNISH

Place a floweret of whipped cream in the center of the soup and decorate the edge of the melon with whipped cream also. Serve immediately.

* Soup may be prepared a day in advance and refrigerated until needed. Do not peel melon until serving time. Stir soup well before pouring into melon shells. Garnish immediately.

MOUSSE AU CHOCOLAT

Here is a dessert that promises to satisfy the most deep-seated chocolate addiction. It's smooth, rich, and delectable. You won't believe anything so good can be so easy to prepare.

INGREDIENTS
½ cup heavy cream
½ cup light cream
½ 4½-ounce box instant
  chocolate pudding
½ cup whipped cream
shavings of semisweet chocolate

ASSEMBLE
mixing bowl
electric mixer; the hand variety
  is best
measuring cup
slotted spoon
4 small earthenware pots

DIRECTIONS

Measure light and heavy cream into mixing bowl. Add instant pudding mix. Beat with hand mixer on slow or stir rapidly with spoon until mix thickens. Spoon ½ cup of whipped cream on top of instant pudding. With slotted spoon, fold in whipped cream by cutting through cream, down into the pudding, then up and over, repeating process until the cream and the pudding are almost but not completely mixed. *Never stir!* Spoon mousse into the small earthenware pots and shave semisweet chocolate onto mousse. Refrigerate until serving time.

GARNISH

Top with ½ candied cherry and 2 pieces candied citron in the shape of a flower with leaves.

CHOCOLATE FONDUE
(serves 2 to 4)

For a luscious dessert that is easy to prepare and a delight to eat, simply dip bits of fruit, cake and/or nuts into this creamy chocolate fondue.

INGREDIENTS

10 ounces Swiss milk chocolate or any high-quality milk chocolate
½ cup heavy cream
¼ cup kirsch
½ cup small ripe strawberries
1 pear, peeled and sliced
½ cup golden raisins
½ cup candied cherries
¼ small angel food cake cut in 1-inch squares
or tangerine sections, miniature creampuffs, nuts, etc.

ASSEMBLE

fondue pot or small chafing dish
measuring cup
stirring spoon
knife
small dishes
fondue forks

DIRECTIONS

Break the chocolate into a fondue pot. Add the cream and melt the chocolate, stirring constantly. Stir in the kirsch and continue to cook for one minute. Serve surrounded by small bowls of tidbits. To eat, spear bits of fruit, etc., with fondue forks and dip into the hot melted chocolate.

PÊCHES MELBA

Serve at a moment's notice—and receive plaudits!

INGREDIENTS

2 poached peach halves (see Your
   Own Freezer Peaches, page 245,
   or, in a pinch, canned peach
   halves will do), drained
½ cup seedless raspberry jelly
1 tablespoon lemon juice
2 scoops vanilla ice cream

ASSEMBLE

blender
measuring cup
set measuring spoons
ice cream scoop
2 small silver or crystal bowls

DIRECTIONS

Measure the jelly and lemon juice into blender container and
blend at low speed for 10 seconds. Place one scoop vanilla ice
cream in each serving dish, top each with a peach half and half
of the raspberry syrup. Serve immediately.

MONT-BLANC

Try this super-sweet, elegant dessert as a perfect aftermath to a French meal . . . or any other, for that matter. The rich chestnut purée is beaten with butter and sugar, then topped with unsweetened whipped cream.

INGREDIENTS

2 tablespoons butter, at room temperature
1 8¾-ounce can sweetened chestnut purée (sometimes called chestnut spread)
1 tablespoon confectioners sugar
½ teaspoon vanilla extract
½ cup heavy cream, whipped
semisweet chocolate
6 candied violets (optional)

ASSEMBLE

electric mixer
can opener
set measuring spoons
2 champagne glasses
stirring spoons

DIRECTIONS

Cream the butter in the small bowl of your electric mixer, then add the purée and beat at low speed until well blended. Beat in the sugar and vanilla. Divide the mixture into champagne or wine glasses. Beat the heavy cream until stiff and heap it over the portions of purée. Refrigerate for at least one hour, or until needed.

To serve, garnish each with shaved semisweet chocolate and top each with 3 candied violets.

STRAWBERRIES ROMANOFF

Very simply—delicious!

INGREDIENTS
2 cups chilled strawberries
⅓ cup granulated sugar
¼ cup very cold freshly squeezed
   orange juice
¼ cup plus 1 tablespoon Cointreau
½ cup very cold heavy cream

ASSEMBLE
colander
measuring cup
set measuring spoons
small mixing bowl
spoon
2 large wineglasses
pastry tube with fluted
   nozzle

DIRECTIONS

Hull the berries, then rinse them in the colander and allow to drain well. Meanwhile, stir together the sugar, juice, and ¼ cup Cointreau. Toss the strawberries with this mixture. Divide the sweetened berries into the wineglasses.

Refrigerate until ready to serve, then beat the cream until stiff, fold in the remaining tablespoon of Cointreau, and pipe points of whipped cream over the berries. Serve immediately.

Drinks

Stir in friendship and serve

These drinks are in a category all by themselves. Each in its own way is special. The emphasis is not on alcoholic content: those recipes can be found in any bartender's guide. These are drinks with that certain flair that proves you care enough about your guests to go out of your way to please them.

In every age, in every part of the world, even in the most primitive of civilizations the warmth of friendship has been considerably heightened by the glow produced from the favorite local brew. Whether it has been made on the sly in the Kentucky hills, filtered through charcoal in the shadow of the Kremlin, or brewed up in some witch doctor's hut, the most important ingredient is not alcohol, but camaraderie.

So it is with the drinks featured here. Hot Buttered Rum and Cider with Spiced Peach, warming when shared with friends after skiing. Cold Brandied Coffee with Ice Cream, cooling when sipped with fellow tennis enthusiasts after the match. Golden Peach Eggnog, festive when toasting in the New Year. Café Diable, really luxurious as a finale for your favorite dinner guests, or Mocha Steamer for you to enjoy if you're a nondrinker.

Brew up these drink recipes, stir in a liberal amount of friendship, and serve. You won't go wrong.

Drinks for occasions

HOT BUTTERED CIDER

A treat for the grown-ups on Halloween, or any crisp autumn evening.

INGREDIENTS
8 tablespoons golden rum
4 teaspoons brown sugar
2 mugs hot cider
2 tablespoons Cointreau
2 teaspoons sweet butter
2 sticks cinnamon
¼ teaspoon allspice
¼ teaspoon powdered cloves

ASSEMBLE
2 mugs; pewter is best
saucepan
set measuring spoons

DIRECTIONS
Pour rum and brown sugar into saucepan. Warm and set aflame. When flame goes out, add remaining ingredients and heat to scalding. Pour into pewter mugs and serve steaming.

HOT BUTTERED RUM AND CIDER WITH SPICED PEACH

Shades of Captain Morgan! Wouldn't he have loved a cup of this to warm his heart on a winter's night? He might have favored a stronger potion of rum, though, and so might you.

INGREDIENTS
8 tablespoons rum
2 pieces of orange peel
4 teaspoons maple syrup
2 teaspoons sweet butter
2 cinnamon sticks
8 cloves
¼ teaspoon allspice
2 tablespoons juice from spiced
  peaches
2 canned spiced peaches
2 cups hot cider

ASSEMBLE
2 pewter mugs
saucepan
set measuring spoons
paring knife
spoon

DIRECTIONS
Warm the rum in saucepan. Place one strip orange peel with one tablespoon warm rum in each pewter mug. Set aflame. When flame goes out add half of the maple syrup, butter, spices, rum, spiced peach syrup, and one spiced peach to each pewter mug. Heat cider to scalding in saucepan and pour over the mixture in the mug. Stir. Serve immediately.

HOT WINE PUNCH

Celebrating the victory of your favorite football team? Bones cold from sitting in the stadium? Throat scratchy from scream-ing the team on? Need something to warm and soothe and start the conversation flowing? Serve this!

INGREDIENTS
1 tablespoon lemon juice
1 tablespoon sugar
1 cinnamon stick
10 whole cloves
1 cup water
½ bottle red Bordeaux

ASSEMBLE
chafing dish or saucepan
Sterno
corkscrew
set measuring spoons
measuring cup

DIRECTIONS
Light flame under blazing pan of chafing dish or under sauce-pan. Add lemon juice, sugar, cinnamon stick, cloves, and water. Bring to boil. Pour in wine and slowly heat. Do not boil. Serve hot.

GOLDEN PEACH EGGNOG
(*serves 4*)

*Your guests as well as your holiday candles will be all aglow if
you whip up this froth of creamy eggnog with mellow peach
brandy and golden rum. Drink the eggnog alone, then gobble
up the peaches with vanilla ice cream and eggnog sauce. Too
good to be true, even on Christmas.*

INGREDIENTS
4 eggs
½ cup sugar
½ cup peach brandy
1 cup golden rum
1 cup cognac
2 cups cold milk
1 cup heavy cream
8 peach halves
2 sticks cinnamon
whipped cream
¼ teaspoon nutmeg
vanilla ice cream

ASSEMBLE
punch bowl with cups
ladle
electric mixer; hand mixer is
    easiest
2 mixing bowls
fork
spoon
measuring cup
set measuring spoons
can opener
paper towels
silver dishes

DIRECTIONS
Separate egg whites from egg yolks, putting yolks in one
mixing bowl and whites in another. Beat the egg yolks with a
fork until they are light and creamy. Add ¼ cup sugar and
continue to mix for one minute. Put egg yolk mixture into
punch bowl. Add peach brandy, rum, and cognac. Beat the egg
whites with the electric mixer until they are stiff. Stir cold milk
and heavy cream into punch. Drain peach halves and set on
paper towels to remove excess moisture. Fold egg whites into
mixture in punch bowl, slide peaches into bottom of punch, and

add stick cinnamon. Decorate top of eggnog with whipped cream. Sprinkle with nutmeg. Serve immediately. Serve the peach halves in small silver dishes with vanilla ice cream and eggnog sauce topped with whipped cream and nutmeg.

Coffee drinks

COLD BRANDIED COFFEE WITH ICE CREAM

Peach ice cream in iced coffee, spiked with peach brandy and topped with whipped cream! Better than an ice cream soda for quenching your summertime thirst.

INGREDIENTS

4 heaping teaspoons instant coffee
2 cups cold water
2 tablespoons peach brandy
2 scoops peach ice cream
   whipped cream
2 pinches instant coffee
2 maraschino cherries

ASSEMBLE

2 very tall glasses
2 soda spoons
2 straws
measuring cup
set measuring spoons
ice cream scoop

DIRECTIONS

Measure 2 teaspoons instant coffee into each glass. Add a little cold water. Stir. Add cold water to within 2 inches of the top of the glass. Stir. Add one tablespoon peach brandy and one scoop ice cream to each glass. Stir. Top with whipped cream. Sprinkle with a small pinch of dry instant coffee. Top with a cherry and serve immediately with a straw and a soda spoon.

IRISH COFFEE

This hearty drink may be called Irish Coffee but it belongs to the world and the world is a happier place for it. Even kissing the Blarney Stone couldn't make the conversation flow more freely than does a round of this mixture of coffee and Irish whiskey.

INGREDIENTS
1½ cups boiling water
4 level teaspoons instant coffee
8 tablespoons Irish whiskey
sugar (optional)
4 tablespoons whipped cream

ASSEMBLE
saucepan
measuring cup
set measuring spoons
2 Irish coffee cups

DIRECTIONS

Boil water. Place instant coffee, whiskey, and boiling water into saucepan. Sugar as desired. Stir. Pour into Irish coffee cups. Top each with two tablespoons whipped cream. Serve immediately.

ICED COFFEE WITH RUM

Here's a long, cold drink, with good strong coffee to make you ambitious, and good smooth rum so you don't care whether you are or not. The ideal hot-weather drink.

INGREDIENTS
½ cup boiling water
2 tablespoons instant coffee
1 cup cold water
2 teaspoons sugar
4 tablespoons rum
8 ice cubes
whipped cream
¼ teaspoon nutmeg

ASSEMBLE
saucepan
2 tall glasses
set measuring spoons
measuring cup
tablespoon

DIRECTIONS
Bring water to boil in saucepan. Stir in instant coffee, cold water, sugar, and rum. Put 4 ice cubes in each glass. Pour coffee mixture over ice so that one inch is left empty at the top of the glass. Top with whipped cream and sprinkle with nutmeg. Serve cold.

CAFÉ DIABLE

This drink can be the show stopper of the meal! Spicy black coffee with orange peel and cloves set aflame with brandy. The devil with caution—serve Café Diable!

INGREDIENTS

thin outer peels of orange and
   lemon, which should be as
   long as possible
3 teaspoons instant coffee
3 cups boiling water
½ cup brandy
10 whole cloves
1 stick cinnamon
6 lumps sugar

ASSEMBLE

chafing dish
Sterno
set measuring spoons
measuring cup
spoon
2 matches
ladle
quart bowl or coffeepot
2 demitasse cups

DIRECTIONS

Stick whole cloves through the lemon and orange peels at one-inch intervals. Light alcohol burner under chafing dish. Mix instant coffee and hot water in bowl or coffeepot. Heat brandy, orange and lemon peels with cloves, cinnamon, and 5 lumps of sugar in chafing dish until sugar is dissolved. Stir occasionally. Heat bowl of ladle over a match or low flame. Dip up a little of the mixture in the ladle. Put one lump of sugar in the ladle and light. Lower flaming ladle into the mixture in the chafing dish. While this is flaming, pour the hot coffee into chafing dish. When flame goes out, ladle coffee into demitasse cups. Serve hot.

MOCHA STEAMER

If you don't drink and you're tired of watching everyone else sipping something delicious, stir up a Mocha Steamer and let your guests be jealous.

INGREDIENTS
8 level teaspoonfuls instant hot
    chocolate
2 level teaspoons instant coffee
8 tablespoons boiling water
1½ cups hot milk
whipped cream
¼ teaspoon chocolate sprinkles
    (optional)

ASSEMBLE
2 coffee mugs
set measuring spoons
measuring cup
small saucepan
teaspoon
teakettle

DIRECTIONS
Light flame under teakettle and boil a little bit of water. Place 4 level teaspoonfuls instant hot chocolate and 1 level teaspoonful instant coffee in each coffee mug. Add 4 tablespoonfuls boiling water to each cup. Stir. Pour the milk into the saucepan. Place over flame. When hot, pour ¾ cup into each mug. Stir. Top each with 2 tablespoons whipped cream. Garnish with chocolate sprinkles and serve immediately.

Lunches, brunches, and midnight snacks

So much for dinner in all its ordered splendor, but what about those unusual or unanticipated occasions that cry for a treatment of their own? Perhaps it's lunch for unexpected guests "just passing through around mealtime," or lunch for that favorite aunt who is in town for a few days and who dotes on your cooking, or a snack for those late, late guests to whom you would like to serve something special, or perhaps just something yummy for yourself when you get hungry at some offbeat hour.

A good rule to remember is that recipes for lunches, brunches, or midnight snacks should be filling but not too heavy, impressive but not too grand. In general, lunches should be more delicate and underdone, midnight snacks more substantial and flamboyant, and the brunches more wholesome, crackling with wake-up flavor and satisfying enough to take the place of the two light meals they replace.

While lunches, brunches, and midnight snacks may seem tricky and unmanageable, especially when combined with the element of surprise, with proper planning they can be doubly rewarding because of the built-in relaxation supplied by the unusual hour and circumstance of their serving.

CREAMY SCRAMBLED EGGS WITH TRUFFLES

An exquisite combination is creamy scrambled eggs with truffles. Serve with champagne for a brunch or midnight supper that won't soon be forgotten.

INGREDIENTS
4 tablespoons sweet butter
2 truffles, diced
4 eggs
2 tablespoons heavy cream
a sprinkle of white pepper and
   salt

ASSEMBLE
chafing dish (or heavy frying
   pan)
mixing bowl
fork
paring knife
set measuring spoons
can opener

DIRECTIONS
In blazer pan of a chafing dish or in the heavy frying pan place the butter. Turn flame on low. Open the can of truffles and chop two of them. Add the truffles to the butter. Meanwhile, beat the eggs thoroughly in the mixing bowl. Add the beaten eggs, the juice from the can of truffles, and the heavy cream to the chafing dish. Stir constantly until eggs are firm but creamy. Never cook eggs until dry. Serve immediately, seasoned to taste with white pepper and salt.

GARNISH *(Optional)*
Slice one truffle in thin slices. Form a flowerlike pattern on the top of the eggs with these slices. Place a cherry tomato in the center of the flower.

EGGS WITH CHERRY TOMATOES

Not pretentious, but really good for a marvelous brunch or a special-treat breakfast. Grilled cherry tomatoes and eggs set on a buttery mound of crumbs make a really toothsome treat.

INGREDIENTS
8 cherry tomatoes
2 pats butter
2 tablespoons bread crumbs
2 eggs
2 pinches thyme
salt and pepper to taste

ASSEMBLE
2 small individual flameproof
    dishes
paring knife
set measuring spoons

DIRECTIONS
Set broiler on high flame. Wash and dry tomatoes. Slice in half. Arrange tomato halves around edge of 2 flameproof dishes. Place pat of butter in center of each dish. Place under broiler flame for one minute. Remove dishes and sprinkle bread crumbs in bottom of each. Break one egg over bread crumbs in each dish. Sprinkle with thyme, salt, and pepper. Place under broiler until eggs set. Serve hot.

ASPARAGUS AND EGG WITH CHEDDAR CHEESE

Tender asparagus spears, fried eggs, and zesty Cheddar cheese combine for a delectable meal.

INGREDIENTS
1 10-ounce package frozen
   asparagus
6 tablespoons butter
2 eggs
2 tablespoons grated Cheddar
   cheese
4 strips pimiento

ASSEMBLE
small saucepan
set measuring spoons
medium-sized skillet
cover for skillet (or aluminum
   foil)
paring knife
2 oblong serving dishes

DIRECTIONS

Cook asparagus according to directions on package. Meanwhile, place butter in skillet. Carefully break eggs into melted butter. Try to keep eggs from running together. Cover skillet. Cook over low heat. Drain asparagus, taking care not to break spears. Arrange asparagus neatly, ½ of the asparagus on each serving plate. Slide fried egg carefully onto each pile of asparagus.

GARNISH

Crisscross egg yolks with pimiento strips. Pour over the eggs and asparagus the melted butter remaining in the skillet. Sprinkle each dish with one tablespoon of grated cheese. Serve immediately.

EGGS FLORENTINE

An egg dish fit for a king. Spinach and poached eggs topped with grated Swiss cheese and popped in the oven for that one moment that makes the difference.

INGREDIENTS
1 10-ounce package chopped
  frozen spinach
4 eggs
3 tablespoons butter
2 tablespoons flour
1 cup milk
8 drops onion juice
2 egg yolks
⅓ cup heavy cream
a dash of nutmeg
3 tablespoons grated Swiss or
  Cheddar cheese

ASSEMBLE
saucepan
small skillet
egg poacher
measuring cup
set measuring spoons
fork
spoon
small bowl
grater
2 individual baking dishes

DIRECTIONS
Set broiler on high heat. Cook frozen spinach according to directions on package. Meanwhile, poach eggs. In skillet, melt butter and stir in flour. Add milk and onion juice and stir until sauce thickens. Beat 2 egg yolks and 2 tablespoons heavy cream in the small bowl. Stir into sauce. Cook over very low flame. Drain spinach and return to saucepan. Add remaining heavy cream and nutmeg. Stir. Cover the bottoms of the two baking dishes with the spinach mixture. Place two poached eggs in each dish and cover each with half of the sauce in the skillet. Sprinkle with grated Swiss cheese and place under broiler until cheese melts and begins to brown. Serve very hot.

SWISS FONDUE

Do as the Swiss do and invite all your friends to dip a piece of crusty roll into this delectable "dunk." The delicate flavors of Swiss cheese, white wine, and cognac literally melt together to form one of the zestiest of late-night snacks.

INGREDIENTS

½ cup light dry white wine
¾ teaspoon flour
¼ pound grated Swiss cheese
¼ teaspoon nutmeg
a dash each of salt and white
   pepper
2 tablespoons cognac or applejack
2 hard rolls

ASSEMBLE

chafing dish
Sterno
measuring cup
set measuring spoons
paring knife
fondue forks
bread basket lined with a
   napkin

DIRECTIONS

Light fire under blazer pan of chafing dish. Add wine and flour. Heat to the boiling point, stirring constantly. With a fork begin to stir the wine as you add the grated cheese a small handful at a time. Each handful of cheese must be completely melted before you add another. When all the cheese is melted and the mixture begins to bubble a little, add the nutmeg, salt, pepper, and cognac or applejack. Stir. Reduce heat to low and keep mixture warm without burning. Meanwhile cut the rolls into bite-size pieces. Each piece of roll should have some crust on it. Serve at once in chafing dish. Dip pieces of roll in mixture. Eat at once.

SAUTÉED PÂTÉ DE FOIE GRAS AND SWISS CHEESE SANDWICHES

Rich, golden sautéed sandwiches filled with pâté de foie gras and melted Swiss cheese, topped with a smooth cheese sauce. Makes an appetizing lunch or late-night snack.

INGREDIENTS

4 tablespoons olive oil
5 tablespoons butter
4 slices white bread
2 slices pâté de foie gras (canned)
1 cup grated Swiss cheese, packaged
2 tablespoons heavy cream
1 egg
1 cup fine bread crumbs
½ cup cream of chicken soup
¼ cup white wine
½ cup heavy cream
1 pinch nutmeg
1 egg yolk

ASSEMBLE

large skillet
small bowl
measuring cup
plate
set measuring spoons
knife
eggbeater
round cookie cutter, 3 inches in diameter
2 serving plates

DIRECTIONS

Place olive oil and 4 tablespoons butter in skillet. Melt over low heat. Meanwhile cut 4 bread slices into rounds with cookie cutter. Cut 2 slices pâté de foie gras. Place on 2 bread rounds. Spread slightly. Measure ½ cup grated Swiss cheese into small bowl with one tablespoon butter and 2 tablespoons heavy cream. Mash together with spoon. Spread Swiss cheese mixture on remaining 2 bread rounds. Make sandwiches by placing together one cheese-spread bread round and one pâté-spread bread round. Beat egg in bowl and place bread crumbs on plate. Dip sandwich first in beaten egg, then in bread crumbs, and sauté in butter and oil over medium heat until golden brown. Turn once. Place on serving plates. Mix together in skillet concentrated cream of chicken soup, white wine, ½ cup of cream, ½ cup grated Swiss cheese, and nutmeg. Stir over medium heat. Meanwhile beat one egg yolk in small bowl. Add 2 tablespoons sauce to egg yolk. Stir. Over a low flame gradually add the egg yolk mixture to the sauce. Stir. Spoon over sandwiches. Serve sandwiches hot with cheese sauce.

LOBSTER À LA NEWBURG

Most fine restaurants feature this gourmet favorite. Too few home cooks do, but now it's easy! For that special treat, serve savory lobster this way.

INGREDIENTS

1 pound cooked lobster meat
2 tablespoons butter
¼ cup sherry
¼ teaspoon flour
¼ teaspoon paprika
2 egg yolks
½ cup heavy cream
1 tablespoon cognac
2 slices toast

ASSEMBLE

skillet
butcher knife
measuring cup
set measuring spoons
mixing bowl
eggbeater
tablespoon

DIRECTIONS

Slice lobster meat into ½-inch slices. Place butter in skillet. When butter is melted add lobster meat, sherry, flour, and paprika. Cook over high heat and stir constantly until sherry is reduced to half its original quantity. Turn flame to low. In mixing bowl beat egg yolks and cream. Pour over lobster meat. Stir until sauce begins to thicken. Do not boil. Add cognac. Cook 30 seconds more. Serve on toast points.

LOBSTER STEW

Try a bowl of this steaming stew as a special treat just for you. Pure ivory cream floats pieces of red-orange lobster meat, golden butter, black pepper, gray-green thyme, and paprika to make a treat for the eye as well as the palate.

INGREDIENTS

4 tablespoons butter
1 pound ready cooked lobster
   meat, fully defrosted
4 drops onion juice
¾ cup clam juice
2 cups milk
1 egg yolk
½ cup heavy cream
½ teaspoon paprika
2 pinches thyme
a dash or two of coarsely ground
   black pepper
2 tablespoons butter

ASSEMBLE

chafing dish (2-quart size)
Sterno
set measuring spoons
measuring cup
small mixing bowl
tablespoon
fork
2 large soup plates

DIRECTIONS

Place 4 tablespoons butter, lobster meat and onion juice in blazer pan of chafing dish. Light flame under blazer pan and cook lobster meat for one minute. Pour clam juice and milk over lobster. Stir. In a small bowl beat the egg yolk and heavy cream together. Gradually add the egg and cream mixture to the blazer pan of the chafing dish, stirring constantly. Do not boil. Sprinkle with paprika, thyme and pepper. Serve immediately with one tablespoon butter floating in each bowl.

WELSH RAREBIT
(Rabbit) with anchovies

A creamy combination of melted cheese, dry mustard, beer and Worcestershire sauce, tawny and delicious. Spoon over toast points, garnish with tomato slices crisscrossed with anchovies, and slide under the broiler for a minute before serving. Made to order for lunches, brunches, or midnight snacks.

INGREDIENTS

2 tablespoons butter
1 cup beer
1½ teaspoons Worcestershire
   sauce
¼ teaspoon dry mustard
4 drops Tabasco sauce
¾ cup grated Cheddar cheese
4 pieces bread
2 slices tomato
2 strips anchovy
2 sprinkles paprika

ASSEMBLE

small skillet
set measuring spoons
measuring cup
toaster
spoon
paring knife
2 individual shallow baking
   dishes

DIRECTIONS

Turn broiler on high. Melt butter in skillet. Add beer, Worcestershire sauce, dry mustard, Tabasco sauce, and grated cheese. Stir. Turn flame to low. Cut 4 slices toast into strips. Stir sauce until cheese is melted and sauce is smooth. Pile 6 toast strips on each baking dish, 3 going one way and 3 the other. Pour Welsh rarebit over toast.

GARNISH

Top each rarebit with a tomato slice crisscrossed with anchovy fillets. Sprinkle with paprika. Place under the broiler for one minute. Serve at once.

CREAMED CRABMEAT AND OYSTERS

If any single dish approaches perfection this one does. Try it.

INGREDIENTS
6 tablespoons butter
3 tablespoons flour
¼ teaspoon parsley flakes
1 cup milk
½ cup grated packaged Cheddar
   or Swiss cheese
¼ cup chicken consommé
½ cup crabmeat, fully
   defrosted
12 fresh shucked oysters, available at your fish store, or 1
   7-ounce can frozen oysters,
   fully defrosted, picked over,
   shell removed
1 egg yolk
4 tablespoons heavy cream
14 stuffed olives

ASSEMBLE
2 medium-sized skillets
set measuring spoons
measuring cup
small mixing bowl
eggbeater
tablespoon
2 individual ovenproof serving
   dishes

DIRECTIONS

Turn broiler on high heat. Melt butter in skillet, add flour, parsley, milk, and grated cheese. Stir until smooth. Meanwhile, place
chicken consommé in the other skillet, then add crabmeat and
oysters to skillet. Heat for one minute. Gently stir oysters and
crabmeat into cheese mixture in other skillet. Beat egg yolk with
heavy cream. Stir into sauce. Heat, being very careful not to boil.
Divide equally in individual ovenproof dishes. Place stuffed
olives at 2-inch intervals around edge of dish. Place under broiler

until top is golden and beginning to brown here and there. Serve immediately.

GARNISH *(Optional)*
Butter 2 slices of toast. Cut off crusts and cut into eighths. Place toast with points up beside each olive around edge of dish. Tuck bits of parsley at the base of each bit of toast. Serve immediately.

Cooking out gourmet style

What is so disappointing as a backyard barbecue gone wrong? Steak, burned on the outside, still frozen on the inside. Hamburgers falling apart and covered with ashes. Baked beans straight from the can and tepid watermelon with a drowned bee floating in the juice. Meals that most people wouldn't dream of serving indoors even for Monday night supper are often foisted on guests under the guise of barbecuing.

How different outdoor gourmet cooking! Juicy pink shrimp, succulent chicken livers, their natural flavors heightened by the delicate smoky taste that can be achieved only by charcoal cooking, showy Baked Butter and Pea Beans with Mushrooms and Bacon—all dressed up and ready to cook when your guests arrive, leaving you free to enjoy not only the company of your friends but your own delicious cooking in luxurious leisure.

BARBECUE SAUCE

You've never tasted porkchops or spare ribs at their very best until you've had them nestled under this piquant barbecue sauce. Try it on oven-baked chicken, porkchops, ham, too. (serves 4)

INGREDIENTS

2 medium-sized onions
4 tablespoons butter
2 teaspoons dry mustard
2 tablespoons Worcestershire
  sauce
2 teaspoons lemon juice
½ cup tomato catsup
½ cup brown sugar
¾ teaspoon salt
8 tablespoons Your Own Freezer
  Green Pepper (see page 235)
8 drops hot sauce or Tabasco
  sauce

ASSEMBLE

paring knife
set measuring spoons
measuring cup
skillet

DIRECTIONS

Peel and chop onion. Place skillet over medium heat. Add butter, then all other ingredients. Stir while sauce boils for 2 minutes. Serve hot over meat or chicken.

SCALLOPS AND CHERRY TOMATOES EN BROCHETTE

Scallops never had it so good! An attractive way to serve an old standby. Tasty and delicious, with a savory charcoal taste. (serves 4)

INGREDIENTS

1 pound bay scallops, washed
   and patted dry
½ cup melted butter
1½ cups grated Parmesan cheese
1 cup bread crumbs
40 cherry tomatoes
½ teaspoon garlic powder
½ teaspoon salt

ASSEMBLE

skillet
strainer
paper towels
measuring cup
set measuring spoons
4 small skewers
pastry brush

DIRECTIONS

Turn broiler on high. Cook scallops in butter for one minute. Add grated Parmesan cheese to bread crumbs. Roll scallops in cheese-bread crumb mixture. Thread skewers alternately with the scallops and cherry tomatoes. Brush with butter in pan. Sprinkle with garlic powder and salt. Cook over hot charcoal fire until browned.

RED RELISII FOR HAMBURGERS*

A sweet and pungent blending of flavors that give hamburgers and hot dogs an excitement they've never had. Whip up a batch and keep it on hand. A real family pleaser.

INGREDIENTS
6 tablespoons butter
1 cup Your Own Freezer
   Onions (see page 237)
1 cup each Your Own Freezer
   Green Peppers and Red
   Peppers (see page 235)
2 teaspoons dry mustard
3 tablespoons Worcestershire
   sauce
1 tablespoon lemon juice
¾ cup tomato catsup
¾ cup brown sugar
1 teaspoon salt
12 drops hot sauce or Tabasco
   sauce
10 whole cloves
1 stick cinnamon
¼ teaspoon ground cloves

ASSEMBLE
skillet
measuring cup
set measuring spoons
paring knife
tablespoon

DIRECTIONS

Put skillet on a medium flame. Add butter, onion and red and green pepper. Stir for one minute. Add the rest of the ingredients and stir until the mixture has boiled for 3 minutes. Serve hot, or fix ahead of time and serve cold. Good either way.

* May be prepared a week in advance and served hot or cold at serving time.

BAKED BUTTER AND PEA BEANS WITH MUSHROOMS AND BACON

(serves 4)

No beans ever come out of a can tasting like this! These baked beans have mushrooms and bacon, green pepper and onion, spices, maple syrup, mustard and catsup. They are special!

INGREDIENTS

1 15-ounce can baked pork and beans
1 14-ounce can butter beans, drained
8 medium mushrooms, sliced
6 slices bacon
1 green pepper
1 onion
½ cup catsup
½ cup mild yellow mustard
⅔ cup maple syrup
1 teaspoon oregano
4 whole cloves
1 bay leaf

ASSEMBLE

saucepan
can opener
paring knife
spoon
earthenware dish

DIRECTIONS

Open cans of baked beans and butter beans. Drain butter beans. Cut bacon slices in half and put in saucepan. Cook over medium-high heat. Meanwhile trim and discard seeds and pith from green pepper. Cut into slices ½-inch wide. Peel and slice onion. Place pepper, mushroom and onion slices in saucepan with bacon and cook until onion is beginning to glaze and bacon is cooked but not crisp. Add all other ingredients. Stir until hot. Serve in earthenware dish.

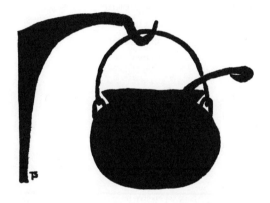

STEAK KEBOBS

The hit of the barbecue! Succulent bite-sized chunks of steak, skewered between tomato, onion, mushroom, and green pepper, and done to a turn over the hot coals of your barbecue pit, or under the broiler, come winter! (serves 4)

INGREDIENTS

1 three-pound sirloin or
    tenderloin steak; have butcher
    remove bone and fat
4 tomatoes
2 large onions
2 green peppers
12 mushroom caps
3 tablespoons olive oil
½ teaspoon garlic powder

ASSEMBLE

pastry brush
butcher knife
can opener
4 skewers

DIRECTIONS

Cut steak into one-inch cubes, trimming fat and gristle. Cut tomatoes into quarters. Peel onion and cut into one-inch wedges. Wash green peppers, remove pulp, and cut into eighths. Thread skewers with alternate pieces of steak, green pepper, tomato, onion, and mushroom caps. Brush with olive oil, sprinkle with garlic powder, and place over hottest part of charcoal fire. Cook two or three minutes, turning frequently. Serve immediately.

PINEAPPLE, SHRIMP, CHICKEN LIVERS AND OLIVES ON SKEWERS

A tempting hors d'oeuvre with enough variety to satisfy any number of guests. Just thread these tasty morsels alternately on skewers, brush with French dressing, sprinkle with nutmeg, and charcoal grill for barbecue cooking that's bound to please. (serves 4)

INGREDIENTS
12 large cooked shrimp
12 canned pineapple chunks
12 chicken livers
12 stuffed olives
½ cup French dressing
ground nutmeg

ASSEMBLE
can opener
4 skewers
measuring cup
pastry brush

DIRECTIONS
Arrange shrimp, pineapple, chicken livers, and olives on skewers. Brush with French dressing. Sprinkle with ground nutmeg. Cook over charcoal fire until slightly brown. Serve immediately.

GINGER-SHRIMP KEBOBS*

These shrimps embellished with ginger, garlic, and soy sauce will be thought special even by seafood connoisseurs. (serves 4)

INGREDIENTS

16 very large raw shrimp
½ cup olive oil
2 teaspoons powdered ginger
2 teaspoons garlic powder
4 tablespoons soy sauce
2 red peppers, cut into 1" x 2" strips
2 green peppers, cut into 1" x 2" strips

ASSEMBLE

pair scissors
paring knife
mixing bowl
measuring cup
set measuring spoons
paper towels
4 skewers

DIRECTIONS

Wash shrimps. Drain on paper towels. Remove shell and vein from shrimp by making cut ¼-inch deep with scissors down entire back of shrimp. In mixing bowl place olive oil, powdered ginger, garlic powder, soy sauce, and shrimp. Stir to coat shrimp thoroughly with sauce. Add pepper strips to shrimp in bowl. Stir. Thread skewers first with red and green pepper strips, then with shrimp. Repeat until skewers are full or until seafood is used up. Broil over very hot charcoal fire, basting with soy sauce mixture from time to time.

* May be prepared several hours in advance. Marinate seafood and red and green peppers in soy sauce and thread on skewers just prior to cooking.

CHICKEN, PINEAPPLE, AND SWEET POTATO KEBOBS

Barbecue cooking, shades of the Old South! These delectable kebobs bring together flavors that were meant for each other. Even the children will love them. (serves 4)

INGREDIENTS
20 chunks uncooked chicken
  meat
1 2-pound can whole sweet
  potatoes
12 slices bacon
20 pineapple chunks
4 tablespoons butter
½ cup maple syrup

ASSEMBLE
butcher knife
small pastry brush
4 skewers
can opener

DIRECTIONS
Cut chicken into one-inch chunks. Remove any skin. Drain sweet potatoes and cut into one-inch chunks. Cut bacon strips in half. Wrap potato chunks in bacon. Alternately thread chicken, pineapple chunks, and bacon-wrapped sweet potatoes on skewers. Melt butter in saucepan and add maple syrup. Brush skewered food with syrup mixture. Broil over most intense heat, basting with syrup from time to time. Turn skewers often. Serve hot.

NOTE
Equally good when cooked under the broiler of your kitchen stove.

CHICKEN LIVERS AND GRAPES

A new combination for barbecue cooking. Soft pink chicken livers charcoal broiled with white grapes. It's the brushing with orange juice concentrate that makes them so delicious. (serves 4)

INGREDIENTS

20 chicken livers

40 white grapes

4 tablespoons frozen orange
   juice concentrated

2 tablespoons oregano

ASSEMBLE

colander

paper towels

pastry brush

can opener

4 long skewers

DIRECTIONS

Wash chicken livers and grapes in colander. Put chicken livers on paper towels to drain. Thread the skewers alternately with chicken livers and grapes. Brush livers and grapes with frozen orange juice concentrate. Sprinkle with oregano. Place over hottest part of charcoal fire. Turn almost constantly until livers are barely cooked. Serve hot and pink.

FRUIT EN BROCHETTE
(serves 4)

Barbecued fruit, brushed with honey and set aflame with brandy: serve over vanilla, rum, or any fruit ice cream to culminate the perfect cookout. (serves 4)

INGREDIENTS

4 fresh ripe peaches
8 fresh apricots
16 maraschino cherries
20 chunks canned pineapple
½ cup honey
½ cup fruit brandy

ASSEMBLE

4 small skewers
measuring cup
pastry brush
paring knife
bowl
paper towels

DIRECTIONS

Wash peaches and apricots. Peel peaches. Thread the fruit on the skewers, beginning and ending with a cherry. Place honey and brandy in bowl. Stir. Brush fruit with this mixture. Cook for a few minutes over charcoal fire. Remove fruit from fire once and brush again with honey-brandy mixture. When fruit is hot and beginning to brown here and there, remove from fire and dribble with brandy. Place skewers back on the fire to ignite the brandy. Serve flaming. Delicious served alone or over vanilla, rum, or any fruit ice cream.

Leftovers

Ugly ducklings transformed

Did you ever look at some particularly tempting bit of leftover food, swear that it was too good to discard, resolve to use it the following day, and instead find yourself throwing it away a few days later?

I'm sure you have and with very good reason. Food that is recooked is seldom tasty. But there are exceptions to every rule and this rule is no exception. Some foods actually taste better when they are served the second day in some new, tempting way. But the usual method of serving leftover food—to merely reheat it (often without the benefit of even a sauce) makes most leftovers limp and tasteless. If there is one thing cooked food doesn't need it is more cooking.

The secret of leftover cooking is very often no cooking at all, as in Asparagus Vinaigrette, Coquilles St. Jacques Salad, Eggs à la Russe, Cold String Bean and Shrimp Salad, Asparagus and Smoked Salmon Salad, or Vegetables à la Grecque. Here precooked food is used as it would be if these recipes were started from scratch. These recipes *call* for cooked food. It's really not like using leftovers at all, so naturally these dishes turn out sparkling and still full of life. In Chicken Princesse and Breast of Chicken Perigourdine, chicken, which would tend to dry out if reheated in any other manner, is placed in a rich sauce and not cooked . . . just warmed enough to taste delicious. For Potato Pflutters, the food to be recooked takes an entirely different form and so retains the brightness and vitality of newly cooked food. The recipes you find in this section may be based on those ugly ducklings of the kitchen, leftovers, but, true to form, at the end of the story those ugly ducklings turn into swans.

Leftover eggs

EGGS À LA RUSSE

Here's a classic found on the most distinguished menus. And so easy to prepare!

INGREDIENTS
½ cup mayonnaise
2 tablespoons chili sauce
½ teaspoon tarragon vinegar
2 drops Tabasco sauce
10 drops lemon juice
2 leftover hard-cooked eggs
2 teaspoons black caviar
2 teaspoons red caviar

ASSEMBLE
small mixing bowl
measuring cup
set measuring spoons
tablespoon
2 small serving plates

DIRECTIONS
Place mayonnaise, chili sauce, vinegar, Tabasco sauce, and lemon juice in mixing bowl. Stir. Peel eggs and cut in half lengthwise. Place 2 egg halves, yolks down, on each serving plate. Cover eggs with sauce. Top one egg half with a teaspoon black caviar, the other with red caviar. Serve cold.

Leftover chicken

BREAST OF CHICKEN PERIGOURDINE

One of the most esoteric of company dishes, using leftover chicken breast. Succulent white chicken meat enhanced with a rich brown Perigourdine sauce spiked with truffles, topped off with a slice of fine pâté de foie gras. Rich and unbelievably delicious!

INGREDIENTS
1 whole chicken breast, cooked
3 tablespoons butter
2 tablespoons Your Own Freezer
   Onions (see page 237)
1 tablespoon flour
1 10½-ounce can beef
   consommé
1 teaspoon truffle juice
2 tablespoons chopped black
   truffle
3 tablespoons tomato sauce
3 tablespoons sherry
1 teaspoon meat extract
2 slices fine pâté de foie gras

ASSEMBLE
skillet
can opener
paring knife
set measuring spoons

DIRECTIONS

Carefully remove meat from bone, keeping breast meat in 2 whole pieces. If necessary, trim uneven edges. Place 3 tablespoons butter in skillet. Add chopped frozen onion. Brown onion *slightly.* Add one tablespoon flour. Stir. Cook until flour is *brown* but not burned. Add consommé, truffle juice, chopped truffle, tomato sauce, sherry, meat extract, and 2 pieces of chicken breast. Boil over high flame for 3 or 4 minutes, stirring occasionally. Do not allow sauce to stick or burn. Place chicken breasts on plate. Top each with three spoons of sauce and one generous slice paté de foie gras. Serve immediately, with extra sauce served separately.

WINE
Bordeaux Graves

CHICKEN PRINCESSE

I guarantee you won't have anything left over but the dish in which you cook this deliciously creamy treat, using leftover chicken and broccoli.

INGREDIENTS	ASSEMBLE
1 10½-ounce can cream of chicken soup	blender
1 cup leftover chicken meat, boned	can opener
	skillet
3 tablespoons heavy cream	set measuring spoons
4 tablespoons sherry	saucepan
1 cup leftover cooked broccoli	grater
10 whole blanched almonds	measuring cup
¼ cup grated Swiss or Cheddar cheese	fork
	paper towels
	shallow ovenproof serving dish
	spoon

DIRECTIONS

Set broiler on high heat. Blend chicken soup for one minute on high speed. Pour into skillet. Add chicken, cream, sherry, and heat. Place broccoli on paper towels to drain for a second. Line bottom of flameproof dish with broccoli and chicken meat. Pour chicken soup mixture over broccoli and chicken. Sprinkle with blanched almonds and grated cheese. Place under broiler for one minute or until cheese is melted and slightly browned. Serve very hot.

NOTE

To serve 4, double amounts of chicken and broccoli only.

GARNISH *(Optional)*

Before placing under broiler, squeeze one cup mashed potato mixed with 2 tablespoons each butter and heavy cream through pastry tube and pipe a ring around edge of dish. Place under broiler until golden brown and serve immediately.

WINE

Moselle (German dry) slightly chilled

Leftover potatoes

BAKED STUFFED CHEESE POTATOES

If you think there's nothing less promising than a cold potato, these cheese-y leftover baked potatoes may change your mind. They're perfect for any occasion.

INGREDIENTS

2 large leftover baked potatoes
2 cloves garlic
½ cup grated cheese
½ teaspoon salt
6 tablespoons milk
2 tablespoons butter
2 tablespoons grated Swiss or
   Cheddar cheese

ASSEMBLE

tablespoon
fork
garlic press
paring knife
electric hand mixer
set measuring spoons
tablespoon
large mixing bowl
measuring cup
small saucepan

DIRECTIONS

Set broiler on high heat. Cut a lengthwise slice from the top of each potato. Scoop out pulp, being careful not to break potato shells. Peel and crush garlic. Place potato pulp, garlic, grated cheese, and salt in the mixing bowl. Mash with fork until fairly smooth. Heat the milk and butter in saucepan, add potato mixture and stir for one minute over high heat. Cream potatoes using hand mixer on high speed. Pile potato high into the potato shells. Press one tablespoon grated cheese onto top of each potato. Place under broiler for one minute. Serve hot.

CLAM HASH*

Here's a wonderful dish using leftover boiled potatoes for an impromptu cold-weather snack.

INGREDIENTS	ASSEMBLE
3 strips bacon	can opener
¾ cup Your Own Freezer Onions (see page 237)	paring knife
	measuring cup
1 7½-ounce can minced clams	set measuring spoons
3 medium-sized leftover boiled potatoes	skillet
	cup
2 teaspoons flour	tablespoon
2 teaspoons butter	slotted spoon
2 teaspoons Worcestershire sauce	
¼ teaspoon salt	
¼ teaspoon pepper	

DIRECTIONS

Cut bacon strips in quarters and fry over high heat for one minute. Lower flame to medium, add onion, and cook until light brown. With slotted spoon, place one can minced clams in skillet. Carefully pour remaining clam liquid into skillet, avoiding any sand which may be present in bottom of can. Peel and chop potatoes. Add to clam mixture. Cook for one minute. Cream flour and butter in cup. Add butter mixture, Worcestershire sauce, salt and pepper to clam hash. Stir over medium heat until slightly thickened. Serve hot.

GARNISH *(Optional)*

Sprinkle with finely chopped parsley, if desired.

* May be prepared several hours in advance if desired. Reheat at serving time.

COQUILLES ST. JACQUES SALAD

A salad unusual in its subtle combination of tastes, using leftover boiled potatoes and scallops. Definitely understated. Definitely gourmet.

INGREDIENTS

¾ cup white wine
2 tablespoons Your Own Freezer
   Onions (see page 237)
2 small leftover potatoes, boiled
   in their jackets, peeled and
   sliced
1 cup cooked scallops
1 egg yolk
¾ cup mayonnaise
1 teaspoon olive oil
4 drops bottled onion juice
½ teaspoon lemon juice
1 tablespoon Your Own Freezer
   Chives (see page 239)

ASSEMBLE

small saucepan
paring knife
measuring cup
large mixing bowl
2 small mixing bowls
wire whisk or fork
set measuring spoons
salad bowl

DIRECTIONS

Bring wine and onion to a boil. Remove from flame. Place sliced potatoes and scallops in large mixing bowl. Pour warm wine and onion over them. In mixing bowl whisk egg yolk until it is creamy. Add mayonnaise, olive oil, onion juice, and lemon juice to egg yolk. Whisk until the mayonnaise is smooth. Drain potatoes and scallops. Mix potatoes and scallops with mayonnaise. Put salad into salad bowl and sprinkle with chives. Serve at room temperature.

POTATO PFLUTTERS

Bound to cause a flutter at dinner are these fluffy little potato pflutters, using leftover mashed potatoes. Puffy, golden brown, and just garlicky enough to please, they're sure to win over guests in a hurry. Even the children will love them!

INGREDIENTS

4 tablespoons hot melted butter
2 cups mashed potatoes
2 egg yolks
½ teaspoon salt
¼ teaspoon nutmeg
1 clove garlic, peeled and
    crushed
4 teaspoons Your Own Freezer
    Parsley (see page 240)

ASSEMBLE

measuring cup
set measuring spoons
fork or electric mixer
spoon
mixing bowl
small saucepan
ovenproof serving dish

DIRECTIONS

Turn broiler flame on high. Melt butter in saucepan. Mix potatoes, egg yolks, and butter together with a fork or electric mixer. When fairly well mixed, add remaining ingredients and mix again. Place spoonfuls of the potato mixture on the greased serving dish and place under broiler for 5 minutes. Serve hot.

Leftover vegetables

ASPARAGUS AND SMOKED SALMON SALAD*

Not complicated but really good, either as a salad or as an attractive addition to a cold dinner menu. Better yet, make half a recipe and try it when you're lunching alone.

INGREDIENTS

4 slices smoked salmon, Alaska or Nova Scotia

12 stalks cold cooked leftover asparagus

2 tablespoons tarragon vinegar

¼ teaspoon salt

4 thin wedges lemon

4 strips pimiento

2 pinches of tarragon

ASSEMBLE

paring knife

set measuring spoons

2 serving plates

DIRECTIONS

Place two slices salmon side by side on each serving plate. If the slices are narrow, place them an inch or two apart so that they will show under the asparagus. On each plate, place 3 spears of asparagus side by side on top of the slices of smoked salmon and facing the same direction. On top of the three spears of asparagus place two spears, then one. Repeat on second plate. Sprinkle each mound of asparagus with one tablespoon vinegar and a little salt.

GARNISH

Cut 4 thin wedges of lemon and 4 strips pimiento. Place one wedge of lemon on either side of the mounds of asparagus. Sprinkle with a pinch of tarragon. Form X of pimiento on each mound of asparagus. Serve cold.

* Can be prepared several hours in advance and refrigerated until needed.

SAUCE VINAIGRETTE FOR USE IN ASPARAGUS VINAIGRETTE*

There are few sauces as tasty as a good vinaigrette sauce, and this one is very good indeed. If you have never tried cold Asparagus Vinaigrette at home where the portions are large and just as you like them, do try! You have a treat in store.

INGREDIENTS

1 scallion, with 3 inches of
   green top
1 large dill pickle
1 hard-cooked egg
¼ cup tarragon vinegar
2½ tablespoons olive oil
2 teaspoons prepared lemon juice
3 teaspoons sugar
½ teaspoon salt
2 tablespoons Your Own Freezer
   Green Pepper (see page 235)

ASSEMBLE

measuring cup
set measuring spoons
paring knife
small mixing bowl
tablespoon

DIRECTIONS

Finely chop scallion, dill pickle, and hard-cooked egg. In mixing bowl blend vinegar, olive oil, lemon juice, salt and pepper, and sugar. Add all remaining ingredients. Serve cold.

* May be prepared 24 hours in advance of serving. Refrigerate until needed.

ASPARAGUS VINAIGRETTE*

INGREDIENTS
14 spears cold cooked asparagus
10 tablespoons Sauce Vinaigrette

ASSEMBLE
set measuring spoons
fork
2 small plates

DIRECTIONS
Arrange asparagus spears on two plates, four spears side by side, three on top of these. Pour 5 tablespoons Sauce Vinaigrette over each stack of asparagus. Serve cold.

GARNISH *(Optional)*
Cut one hard-cooked egg in slicer. Cut 4 long strips pimiento. Press one egg yolk through a fine sieve onto a paper napkin. Place slice of hard-cooked egg on the center of each mound of asparagus. Top each egg slice with teaspoon of hard-cooked egg yolk and one caper. Place one strip of pimiento across the tips of the asparagus and one across base end. Repeat on second plate. Serve cold.

* May be prepared 24 hours in advance of serving. Refrigerate until needed.

SPINACH SALAD

Everyone knows hard-cooked eggs and spinach make a wonderful team, but if the spinach is uncooked and anchovies are added, the team becomes unbeatable.

INGREDIENTS

4 cups raw spinach leaves, loosely
   packed
8 anchovy fillets
¼ cup prepared Italian dressing;
   6 tablespoons olive oil and 3
   tablespoons white wine
   vinegar may be substituted
   if desired
2 leftover hard-cooked eggs,
   chopped
2 leftover hard-cooked eggs, cut
   in quarters
8 strips pimiento

ASSEMBLE

colander
paper towels
paring knife
measuring cup
salad bowl
2 salad plates

DIRECTIONS

Wash spinach thoroughly and remove stems. Drain in colander. Pat dry with paper towels. Break spinach into bite-sized pieces and arrange in salad bowl. Drain anchovy fillets on a paper towel. Cut into fourths and add to salad bowl. Pour dressing over salad. Toss. Serve cold.

GARNISH

Sprinkle with finely chopped hard-cooked eggs. Arrange 8 quarters of hard-cooked eggs around edge of bowl, points toward center. Decorate each egg quarter with 1 small strip pimiento. Serve cold.

COLD STRING BEAN AND SHRIMP SALAD*

Can't think of anything less interesting than a cold, cooked, leftover green bean? Try it with cold cooked shrimp, hard-cooked eggs, and French dressing!

INGREDIENTS

8 large cold cooked shrimp,
   peeled and cleaned
1 cup cold leftover green beans
4 cold hard-cooked eggs
⅓ cup cold French dressing
7 black olives

ASSEMBLE

large mixing bowl
measuring cup
paring knife
sieve
salad fork and spoon
salad bowl

DIRECTIONS

Slice the shrimp in half lengthwise. Place the green beans and the shrimp in the mixing bowl. Halve the hard-cooked eggs and slice the whites into thin strips. Add the sliced egg whites and the French dressing to the shrimp and beans. Toss and place in the salad bowl.

GARNISH

Put the egg yolks through a sieve, then sprinkle them over the salad as a garnish. Form a pinwheel of 5 shrimp in the center of the bowl, place one black olive in the center of the shrimp pinwheel and one in the curve of each shrimp used for decoration. Serve cold.

* May be prepared several hours early. Garnish immediately before serving.

VEGETABLES À LA GRECQUE*

Using leftover cauliflower, zucchini. (Green beans, mixed vegetables, lima beans may be substituted or added.) These sparkling bright cooked vegetables, served refreshingly cold, are crisp, succulent, delicious and guaranteed to please even the confirmed vegetable hater. A marvelous addition to Hors d'Oeuvres Variés or Hors d'Oeuvres tray.

INGREDIENTS

8 small white cooked onions

1 3-ounce can mushroom caps

4 artichoke hearts (the smaller
  the better)

½ cup leftover cooked
  cauliflower

½ cup leftover zucchini

4 tablespoons olive oil

2 tablespoons lemon juice

½ teaspoon salt

⅛ teaspoon black pepper

2 cloves garlic

2 sprigs parsley

1 teaspoon chopped chervil

ASSEMBLE

small mixing bowl

large mixing bowl

can opener

garlic press

paring knife

2 forks

paper towels

serving plate

DIRECTIONS

All ingredients should be cold. Open cans or jars of white
onions, mushroom caps and artichoke hearts. Drain all vegetables, measure, and place in large mixing bowl. Measure
olive oil, lemon juice, salt, and black pepper into small
mixing bowl. Peel garlic cloves. Crush in garlic press over
bowl. Add to olive oil. Mix well. Pour olive oil mixture over
vegetables. Toss lightly with 2 forks. Arrange on serving
plate. Wash and chop parsley. Sprinkle parsley and chervil
over salad. Serve cold.

NOTE

Serves 2 or 3.

* May be prepared 24 hours in advance and kept in refrigerator until
needed.

Sauces

"La sauce c'est tout"

If there is any one thing that separates the true gourmet cook from the chintz-and-ruffles housewife cook, it is the appreciation of sauces.

Now, don't let that frighten you away. You don't have to invent the sauces. You just have to understand them. Once you understand them you will appreciate them, and once you appreciate them, almost automatically your cooking will be transformed. It sounds simple and it is meant to be.

The first thing to understand about gourmet sauces is this. With the exception of white sauces, they seldom use flour. Where thickening is desired, it is nearly always obtained by using egg yolks or, in the case of meat sauces, by reduction in quantity through cooking.

Second, sauces, while of supreme importance in flavor, are invariably used sparingly.

Third, the gourmet sauce is subtle in flavor even at its richest.

It takes a practiced palate indeed to decipher the subtleties in a French sauce, but most often you can count on the following: (1) light sauce contains heavy cream, butter in quantity, white wine, brandy, veal or chicken stock, and those wizards, shallots. An onion can be substituted for shallots, but try to avoid this if you possibly can. (2) A golden sauce is a light sauce thickened with egg yolks. (3) A brown sauce nearly always contains meat juices, red or white wine, shallots, and parsley. (4) Basic white sauces contain milk, flour, butter, and salt.

Even the variations have their rules: Spanish sauces almost always contain olive oil, onion, tomato, green pepper, and garlic.

Creole sauces mimic French and Spanish sauces, but often with olives or okra added. Hawaiian sauces most often contain soy sauce, ginger, and pineapple.

In France (Sauce Heaven) they say, "La sauce c'est tout"— "The sauce is all." Whether it is an invisible cloak of flavor, or lies in folds as rich and smooth as brown silk velvet, the truth is in the tasting. "La sauce c'est tout!"

MEXICAN CURRY SAUCE

A stunning sauce with more built-in "sit up and take notice"
than a string of firecrackers. Serve this with leftover chicken,
lamb, shrimp, crabmeat, or hard-cooked eggs, add a little rice,
and watch a four-star meal appear out of almost nothing.

INGREDIENTS
3 tablespoons cooking oil
6 tablespoons Your Own Freezer
  Onions (see page 237)
¾ tablespoon curry powder
1 tablespoon flour
½ teaspoon salt
1 cup milk
3 tablespoons chopped red
  pimiento
6 tablespoons Your Own Freezer
  Green Pepper (see page 235)

ASSEMBLE
skillet
set measuring spoons
measuring cup
small saucepan
paring knife

DIRECTIONS
In a skillet heat oil over medium-high flame. Add onions and
cook until brown. Do not burn. Stir curry powder, flour and
salt into the onions. Pour milk into the onion mixture. Stir
rapidly until smooth. Add green pepper and pimiento to the
curry sauce. Boil rapidly for 2 minutes. Serve with leftover
chicken or meat (preferably lamb).

CREOLE SAUCE

A sauce like this can transform the plainest meat or poultry. If you can't get away for a trip to New Orleans, have a sip of this sauce instead. Try it on flounder or halibut or leftover chicken or pot roast. Equally good over all.

INGREDIENTS
2 tablespoons butter
3 tablespoons each Your Own
   Freezer Onions and Your
   Own Freezer Green
   Peppers (see page 237
   and 235)
10 mushrooms, peeled and sliced
10 stuffed green olives, sliced
¼ cup beef consommé
¼ cup water
1 cup stewed tomatoes
¼ teaspoon thyme
1 bay leaf
12 clove garlic, peeled and
   crushed
1 tablespoon sherry

ASSEMBLE
skillet
set measuring spoons
paring knife
can opener
tablespoon
blender
strainer

DIRECTIONS
Place skillet over medium-high flame. Add butter and 3 tablespoons each green peppers and onion. Sauté this while you peel and slice 10 mushrooms. Add mushrooms. Slice 10 olives into circles. Add olives, consommé, and water. Stir. Place one cup of stewed tomatoes in container of blender. Cover and blend on high speed for 30 seconds. Pour tomatoes through a strainer into the skillet. Stir with a spoon to force most of the tomato pulp through. Add thyme, bay leaf, garlic, and sherry. Boil. Serve hot.

SAUCE MADRID

Here's a cold seafood sauce with enough zing to open any eye. As a special treat, marinate cooked shrimp in it overnight. Serve as one of a selection of cold hors d'oeuvres. Marvelous.

INGREDIENTS
1 tablespoon chopped celery
1 tablespoon minced scallion
2 teaspoons Your Own Freezer
   Parsley (see page 240)
½ cup olive oil
5 tablespoons wine vinegar
3 tablespoons cognac
1 tablespoon lemon juice
3 tablespoons chili sauce
1 tablespoon horseradish
2 teaspoons Your Own Freezer
   Chives (see page 239)
½ teaspoon dry mustard
1 egg yolk
a pinch each salt and pepper

ASSEMBLE
medium-sized mixing bowl
measuring cup
paring knife
set measuring spoons
wire whisk or slotted spoon

DIRECTIONS
Place all ingredients in mixing bowl. Mix thoroughly with wire whisk or slotted spoon. Serve cold. Delicious over cold seafood, especially shrimp.

HAWAIIAN STEAK SAUCE

Tired of steak the same old way? Looking for a marinade that's really good? Here it is, with many thanks to the Islands for dreaming it up.

INGREDIENTS
⅓ cup soy sauce
¼ teaspoon powdered ginger
¼ cup pineapple juice
½ teaspoon sugar
2 cloves garlic

ASSEMBLE
mixing bowl
set measuring spoons
measuring cup
garlic press

DIRECTIONS
Stir all ingredients except garlic together in mixing bowl. Peel garlic and crush over mixing bowl. Scrape bottom of garlic press to obtain as much garlic as possible. Stir and use for marinating or as a barbecue sauce for outdoor grilling.

HOLLANDAISE SAUCE

The most beautiful sauce of all. Hollandaise sauce can now be made with the twirl of a blender. Marvelous for dressing up broccoli, asparagus, artichoke bottoms, hard-cooked eggs, breast of chicken or fish.

INGREDIENTS
1 cup hot water
3 egg yolks
2 teaspoons lemon juice
pinch of salt and white pepper
½ cup sweet butter

ASSEMBLE
blender
cup
set measuring spoons
measuring cup
small saucepan

DIRECTIONS

Pour hot water into blender. Let stand one minute. Meanwhile separate 3 egg yolks and put in a cup. Empty blender. Put egg yolks, lemon juice, salt, and pepper into blender. Cover. Turn blender on high speed for a few seconds. Turn off. Melt ½ cup butter in saucepan. While butter is very hot, partially cover blender; turn on high and add butter in a steady stream. Do not pour in butter too rapidly. As soon as butter is completely added, turn off blender motor. Serve immediately.

HERB-MINT SAUCE

A subtle sauce. Try it spooned over cooked fish or broccoli for a dish that will delight you.

INGREDIENTS
1 cup hot water
2 tablespoons butter
1 egg yolk
2 tablespoons dry sauterne
1 tablespoon light cream
1 teaspoon tarragon (dried)
2 pinches each of crushed sweet
   basil, rosemary, nutmeg,
   thyme, salt and pepper
¼ teaspoon mint flakes

ASSEMBLE
double boiler
corkscrew
set measuring spoons
wire whisk or tablespoon
table knife

DIRECTIONS
Pour one cup hot water into bottom of double boiler. Place over medium-high flame. Place the top of the double boiler over the bottom half. Then add butter, egg yolk, sauterne, and light cream. Beat with the wire whisk until the sauce begins to thicken. Add tarragon, salt, pepper, sweet basil, rosemary, thyme, and mint. Continue to whisk for two minutes.

COCONUT CREAM SAUCE

This Coconut Cream Sauce made from sweet cream, sour cream, and cream cheese is creamy three ways. Serve over any cold, sweetened fruit. Fresh blackberries or figs are best.

INGREDIENTS
2 ounces cream cheese
4 tablespoons heavy cream
¼ cup sour cream
5 tablespoons grated coconut

ASSEMBLE
mixing bowl
measuring cup
set measuring spoons
fork
tablespoon

DIRECTIONS
Place cream cheese and sweet cream in mixing bowl. Mash with fork, then stir rapidly until cream cheese is soft and creamy. Add sour cream. Mix, then beat until smooth. Add grated coconut. Stir. Serve cold.

MORNAY SAUCE

One of the hardest-working of all the classic French sauces. Tuck almost anything under a mantle of Mornay, sprinkle it with grated Swiss cheese, put it under a broiler for a minute, and voila!—a creation worthy of the finest cook.

INGREDIENTS
1 cup milk
3 tablespoons butter
3 tablespoons flour
6 drops onion juice
¼ teaspoon parsley flakes
½ cup grated Cheddar or Swiss cheese, packaged
2 pinches ground nutmeg
1 egg yolk
4 tablespoons heavy cream
salt and pepper to taste
2 tablespoons whipped cream

ASSEMBLE
skillet
set measuring spoons
small saucepan
measuring cup
small mixing bowl
eggbeater
tablespoon

DIRECTIONS
Heat milk over high flame until scalding hot. Melt butter in skillet. Stir in flour, onion juice, parsley flakes, Cheddar or Swiss cheese, 2 pinches of nutmeg, and scalded milk. Stir until the cheese is melted and the sauce is smooth. In a bowl beat together the egg yolk and the heavy cream. Stir into sauce. Add salt and pepper to taste. Cook until sauce is smooth and thick. Be careful not to boil. Fold in the whipped cream. Especially good with shrimp, chicken, crabmeat, oysters, eggs, broccoli, spinach, etc., etc., etc.

SWEET AND MUSTARD-Y DIPPING SAUCE

The most delectable dip I know of takes a mere 45 seconds to prepare. Serve as a dunk for hors d'oeuvres or plan a special lunch around it: 1½-inch chunks of cheese and cold sausage, mound these on a large cheeseboard. Serve with this savory dip and a tempting bowl of hot or cold soup.

INGREDIENTS

1 11-ounce jar peach butter
   or jam
4 tablespoons mild yellow
   mustard

ASSEMBLE

small bowl
set measuring spoons
mixing spoon

DIRECTIONS

Mix peach butter and mustard thoroughly in a small bowl. Serve at room temperature.

APRICOT SAUCE

This sauce is marvelous when heated and served over roast pork, chicken, game or ham. For a complete about-face, serve hot over vanilla or peach ice cream. Versatile, isn't it?

INGREDIENTS
1 7¾-ounce jar strained apricots
   for babies
2 tablespoons Grand Marnier or
   Cointreau
4 tablespoons butter
1 teaspoon honey

ASSEMBLE
jar opener
set measuring spoons
small saucepan or skillet
spoon

DIRECTIONS
Place all ingredients in saucepan. Bring to a boil over medium flame. Boil gently for 3 minutes, stirring constantly.

NOTE
3 tablespoons undiluted consommé may be added if less sweetness is desired when serving with meat.

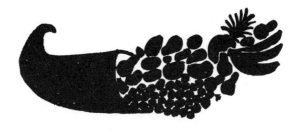

RASPBERRY SAUCE

Berry meets berry in a tempting new way when Raspberry Sauce is poured over fresh, ripe strawberries. Or, for a traditional treat, make Pêches Melba in a minute by pouring this sauce over vanilla ice cream set on half a peach.

INGREDIENTS
½ 10-ounce package frozen
   raspberries, defrosted
1 tablespoon raspberry jelly

ASSEMBLE
blender
set measuring spoons
fine sieve
bowl

DIRECTIONS
Place berries in container of blender. Turn on high speed for one minute. Strain into bowl. Add 1 tablespoon raspberry jelly. Stir until smooth. Serve cold.

CHOCOLATE SAUCE

You'll be known for your chocolate sauce one minute after you serve this. Really good chocolate sauces are rare. Now you are the possessor of one of the most luscious. Bon appétit!

INGREDIENTS

2 squares bitter chocolate
1 tablespoon butter
½ cup sugar
½ cup light cream
½ teaspoon vanilla extract

ASSEMBLE

small heavy skillet
tablespoon
set measuring spoons
mixing bowl
measuring cup

DIRECTIONS

Place chocolate squares and butter in small heavy skillet. Melt chocolate over low flame. In mixing bowl combine sugar and cream. Add to melted chocolate. Stir over medium-low flame until sauce reaches boiling point. Reduce heat. Cook over low flame until sauce thickens slightly. Stir in vanilla. Serve hot or cold.

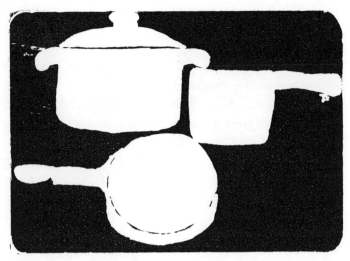

Freezer recipes

Prepare and freeze uncooked vegetables in small amounts because these do not keep as well as cooked vegetables.

YOUR OWN FREEZER GREEN AND RED PEPPERS

INGREDIENTS
2 green or red peppers

ASSEMBLE
sharp knife
paper towels
cookie sheet
aluminum foil
freezer containers

DIRECTIONS
Select firm, crisp peppers. Wash and dry them well, then cut away the white pith and seeds. Cut peppers into small pieces or chop them coarsely. Press out excess moisture with paper towels.

Meanwhile, line a cookie sheet with aluminum foil. Spread the pepper pieces in a shallow layer over the foil. Cover the peppers with another piece of foil and tuck the ends under tightly. Freeze at o degrees F. or below. When frozen, scoop pepper pieces quickly into plastic freezer containers and return to the freezer. Use as called for in your recipe. Loosen the pepper pieces with a fork, measure the amount needed, and refreeze the remainder immediately.

YOUR OWN FREEZER ONIONS

INGREDIENTS
2 medium-sized onions

ASSEMBLE
sharp knife
paper towels
cookie sheet
aluminum foil
freezer container

DIRECTIONS
Peel the onions, chop them coarsely, then spread them on paper towels to soak up excess moisture. Line a cookie sheet with aluminum foil and arrange the onion pieces in a shallow layer over the foil. Cover the onions with a second piece of foil, tucking in the ends tightly. Freeze immediately at 0 degrees F.

When frozen, scoop the onion pieces into a plastic container and return to freezer until needed. Use as called for in your recipe. Loosen the onion pieces with a fork, measure the amount called for in the recipe and refreeze the remainder immediately.

YOUR OWN FREEZER SHALLOTS

INGREDIENTS
½ pint shallots

ASSEMBLE
sharp knife
paper towels
cookie sheet
aluminum foil
freezer container

DIRECTIONS
Prepare according to directions for Your Own Freezer Onions.

YOUR OWN FREEZER CHIVES

INGREDIENTS
fresh chives

ASSEMBLE
paper towels
sharp knife or scissors
cookie sheet
aluminum foil
freezer containers

DIRECTIONS

Wash the chives thoroughly and drain on paper towels until all moisture is absorbed. Mince the chives with a sharp knife or cut them into tiny bits with your kitchen scissors. Arrange the chives in a thin layer on a foil-lined cookie sheet. Cover with a second piece of foil, tucking the ends under tightly. Freeze immediately at o degrees F. or below. Scoop the frozen chives quickly into a freezer container, taking care not to defrost them, and store in the freezer. To use in a recipe, loosen the pieces with a fork, measure amount needed, and refreeze remainder immediately.

YOUR OWN FREEZER PARSLEY

INGREDIENTS
fresh parsley

ASSEMBLE
paper towels
sharp knife or scissors
cookie sheet
aluminum foil
freezer container

DIRECTIONS

Rinse the parsley thoroughly under running water, then drain on paper towels until all moisture is absorbed. Mince the parsley with a sharp knife, or cut the leaves into tiny pieces with your kitchen scissors. Line the cookie sheet with aluminum foil and spread the parsley in a thin layer over the foil. Cover tightly with another piece of foil, tucking the ends under. Freeze immediately at o degrees F. or below. Scoop the frozen parsley quickly into a freezer container, taking care not to defrost it, and store in the freezer. To use in a recipe, loosen the parsley with a fork, measure the amount needed, and refreeze the remainder immediately.

YOUR OWN FREEZER TOMATO PUREE

INGREDIENTS
8 ripe tomatoes
3 tablespoons water

ASSEMBLE
sharp knife
skillet
stirring spoon
strainer
deep bowl
2 freezer containers

DIRECTIONS

Rinse the tomatoes, then dip them briefly in boiling water to loosen the skins. Peel each tomato, cut it in quarters, and shake out the seeds. Chop the pulp coarsely and place in a skillet. Add the water and cook over low heat, stirring constantly, until most of the juice has evaporated. Pour the cooked tomato into the strainer set over the bowl and use the spoon to force the pulp through.

Pour the tomato purée into the plastic containers and freeze at once at 0 degrees F. or below. To use, place the plastic container in a bowl of warm water until the purée softens enough around edges to be removed to the cooking pan.

YOUR OWN FREEZER RICE

Your Own Freezer Rice is easy to prepare and tastes far better than the commercially prepared "quick" variety.

INGREDIENTS
1 cup long-grained rice
water

ASSEMBLE
medium-sized saucepan
strainer
freezer containers

DIRECTIONS
Cook the rice according to package directions, but reduce the cooking time by 10 minutes. Pour the rice into a strainer and rinse under cold running water; drain thoroughly, then spread on paper towels to dry for 30 minutes. Divide the rice into 4 containers and immediately freeze at 0 degrees F. or below.

DIRECTIONS for preparing one container of rice (enough to serve two) To serve the rice, bring ¾ cup salted water to a boil. Add the frozen rice. Cover and allow the water to reach a second boil, then reduce the heat and cook for one minute. Drain well and serve at once, or spoon into a heatproof dish and keep warm in a 250-degree oven until serving time.

YOUR OWN FREEZER MUSHROOMS

INGREDIENTS
½ pound fresh mushrooms
3 tablespoons butter

ASSEMBLE
paper towels
sharp knife
medium-sized skillet
plastic containers

DIRECTIONS
Wipe the mushrooms with a damp cloth and dry on paper towels. (Fresh white mushrooms need not be rinsed unless they are dirt-spattered.) Heat the butter in a skillet over low flame. Cut the mushrooms in half* and cook them slowly in the butter until they begin to brown slightly and most of the liquid cooks away. Cool the mushrooms, then place in plastic containers along with the butter from the pan. Freeze quickly at o degrees F. or below. Keep frozen until needed. To use in a recipe, set the plastic container in a bowl of warm water just long enough to soften the butter so the mushrooms may be easily removed.

* To freeze mushroom caps, remove and chop or slice the stems. Cook and freeze caps and stems separately.

YOUR OWN FREEZER GARLIC TOAST

INGREDIENTS

1 French bread
2 tablespoons butter
3 tablespoons vegetable oil
2 garlic cloves, peeled and
   crushed

ASSEMBLE

knife
garlic press
large skillet
cookie sheet
aluminum foil
heavy plastic bag

DIRECTIONS

Cut the bread in slices about ½ inch thick. Heat the butter and oil in the skillet, stir in the garlic, and sauté one minute. Dip both sides of each slice quickly in the garlic butter and sauté the bread until golden brown on each side, turning once.

Meanwhile, line the cookie sheet with aluminum foil. Remove toast from the skillet, cool them and arrange in a single layer over the foil. Cover with another piece of foil, tucking the ends carefully under. Freeze at 0 degrees F. When frozen, remove the garlic toast from the foil, place in a heavy plastic bag, then twist the top to force out excess air and secure with wire fasteners. Return to freezer. Defrost and use as needed, with or without further heating.

Fancy Cheese Croutons for Soup (see page 127) may be frozen in a similar manner. Merely omit anchovies, pimiento and capers.

YOUR OWN FREEZER PEACHES

INGREDIENTS
1 quart water
juice of 2 lemons
7 cups granulated sugar
9 ripe, fresh peaches

ASSEMBLE
large saucepan
measuring cup
wooden spoon
freezer containers
freezer wrap

DIRECTIONS

Bring the water to a boil. Add the juice of 2 lemons, then stir in the sugar, stirring constantly until the sugar dissolves. Peel the peaches, dipping them briefly in boiling water first to loosen the skins. Cut the peaches in half, remove the pits, and set the fruit into the freezer containers, cut side down, 2 or 4 halves to a container, depending on its size.

Pour enough of the hot syrup into each container to completely cover the peach halves, leaving one inch of head space between the level of the liquid and the top of the container. Arrange crushed pieces of freezer wrap over the peaches to keep them immersed in the syrup. Cool quickly and freeze at 0 degrees F. Use as needed.

Menus

The perfect companions

In a book where many things have been made much of, it may seem contradictory to say that menu making is *the* most important aspect of serving a really superb meal. If you think back on what has preceded, however, you will remember that one of the first statements made in this book was ". . . cooking is easy. If you can read, you can cook." This being true, it will not seem amiss to emphasize the prominent role menus play in the art of feeding yourself and your guests not only properly but expertly.

It may help to remember the following:

1. *The entrée*

Should be selected first.

Should take into consideration the preferences or prejudices of your guests if known to you.

Should be consistent with the time of the year. Serve lighter foods in summer or smaller portions of richer foods.

Should be appropriate for the occasion. The more important the occasion, the more elaborate the meal and the more carefully constructed the menu.

2. *Hors d'oeuvres*

Should complement the entrée both in texture and flavor.

Should not overpower the main course in quantity, flavor, or flamboyance, or you may find the rest of your meal anticlimactic.

Should be impressive enough in taste and appearance to draw the attention of your guest or guests away from animated political or business discussions. Dinner is much more enjoyable if conversation is lively but not too controversial and disturbing.

3. *The soup*

Should contain elements complementary to both the hors d'oeuvre and the entrée.

Should provide a change of pace. If hors d'oeuvre and entrée are attention getters, the soup should be soothing and restful to prepare the way for the main course. On the other hand, if the hors d'oeurve and entrée are rich but bland, the soup should have sufficient personality to open eyes and alert palates for the coming treat. But again, caution!: the main course is still the star!

4. *The salad*

Should offer a change of flavor and texture to heighten the pleasure of the main course. As the soup prepares the palate for the main course, so the salad cools, refreshes, and offers a change of pace during the meal itself. It should therefore complement the flavors of the entrée and offer a stimulating taste change without completely submerging the subtleties of the main course.

5. *The vegetable*

Should be tasteful to supplement and round out the meal as well as to provide an interesting taste treat.

Should be completely subservient to the entrée. Not too similar to, not too different from the main course. If your choice of vegetables is perfect, they will be greatly enjoyed but seldom remembered. Your guest should be so blinded by the beauty of the main course that while relishing every bite of vegetable, he or she is hard put to remember exactly what it was that seemed so delightful.

6. *The dessert*

Should be the only element in the meal that can rival the entrée.

Should still rely upon the main course for inspiration. Although the dessert can be a marvelous attention getter, it must be chosen to complement the meal it follows. A delicate meal relying upon subtlety for its impact can afford to close with a creamy, sensuous dessert. However, a meal rich in its textures and flavors seems to cry out for a light, fruity dessert such as Pêches Flambées. Desserts can be dramatic and different, but must be perfectly suited to the meals they conclude.

BRUNCHES

The following combinations are ideal for brunch!

I.
Curried Pineapple Slices
Creamy Scrambled Eggs with Truffles
Toast Points

II.
Glazed Apple Slices
Greek Pontica

III.
Chilled Tomato Juice with Pepper
Clam Hash

IV.
Chilled Clam Juice
Eggs with Cherry Tomatoes
Rye Toast Points

V.
Strawberry Orange Juice
Apple Pancake

VI.
Fried Bananas
Fluffy Corn Fritters
(with Maple Syrup)

LUNCIIES

(Lunch is generally served with an hors d'oeuvre *or* soup)

Chicken Princesse

May be served with a choice of the following

HORS D'OEUVRES:
Eggs à la Russe
Fresh Mushrooms in Double Cream

SOUPS:
Garlic Soup with Croutons and Poached Egg
Tomato Crab Bisque
Curried Lemon Soup
Jellied Madrilène in Avocado Shells
Chilly Crème de Menthe Soup

SALADS:
Cucumber Salad Damascus
Cauliflower Salad

VEGETABLES:
Carrots and White Grapes
New Peas with Mint
Cauliflower with Almonds
Potato Pflutters
Artichokes with Foie Gras

GO WITHS:
Grilled Cheese Tomatoes
Petite Peas in Artichoke Bottoms
Curried Pineapple Slices

DESSERTS:
Pêches Flambées
Apple Cointreau Sundae
Strawberry Trifle
Sherbet in Orange Cups

Lobster Salad
May be served with a choice of the following:

HORS D'OEUVRES:
Fresh Figs and Walnuts in Prosciutto Ham
Fresh Vegetables with Tuna Dip

SOUPS:
Jellied Madrilène in Avocado Shells
Tomato Crab Bisque
Curried Lemon Soup
Chilly Crème de Menthe Soup

GO WITHS:
Ham Cornucopias
Anchovies in Cherry Tomatoes

DESSERTS:
Pêches Flambées
Apple Pancake
Apple Cointreau Sundae
Cherries Jubilee Sundae
Strawberry Trifle
Greek Pontica
Sherbet in Orange Cups
Mousse au Chocolat

Asparagus and Egg with
Cheddar Cheese
   May be served with a choice of the following:

HORS D'OEUVRES:
   Vegetables à la Grecque
   French Vegetables with Tuna Dip

SOUPS:
   Jellied Madrilène in Avocado Shells
   Tomato Crab Bisque

SALADS:
   Cauliflower Salad
   Bibb Lettuce with Antipasto Dressing

VEGETABLES:
   Garlic Cherry Tomatoes
   Green Beans Serbian
   Vegetables in Cream
   Green Beans au Beurre
   Potato Pflutters
   Baked Stuffed Cheese Potatoes

GO WITHS:
   Grilled Stuffed Cheese Potatoes
   Anchovies in Cherry Tomatoes

DESSERTS:
   Apple Cointreau Sundae
   Greek Pontica
   Sherbet in Orange Cups

Sautéed Pâté de foie gras and
Swiss Cheese Sandwich
   May be served with a choice of the following:

HORS D'OEUVRES:
   Fresh Mushrooms in Double Cream
   Fresh Figs and Walnuts in Prosciutto Ham
   Fresh Vegetables with Tuna Dip

SOUPS:
   Garlic Soup with Croutons and Poached Egg
   Jellied Madrilène in Avocado Shells
   Tomato Crab Bisque
   Curried Lemon Soup
   Gazpacho

SALADS:
   Cucumber Salad Damascus
   Fruit and Cucumber Salad
   Cauliflower Salad
   Caesar Salad
   Cold String Bean and Shrimp Salad
   Coquilles St. Jacques Salad

GO WITHS:
   Anchovies in Cherry Tomatoes
   Grilled Cheese Tomatoes
   Petite Peas in Artichoke Bottoms
   Curried Pineapple Slices

DESSERTS:
   Pêches Flambées
   Apple Cointreau Sundae
   Sherbet in Orange Cups
   Mousse au Chocolat

Mozzarella in Carrozza
   May be served with a choice of the following:

HORS D'OEUVRES:
   Italian Antipasto
   Fresh Figs and Walnuts in Prosciutto Ham
   Fresh Vegetables with Tuna Dip

SOUPS:
   Garlic Soup with Croutons and Poached Egg
   Tomato Crab Bisque
   Gazpacho

SALADS:
   Italian White Bean and Anchovy Salad
   Caesar Salad
   Onion Salad
   Cucumber Salad Damascus
   Cauliflower Salad
   Asparagus and Smoked Salmon Salad

GO WITHS:
   Anchovies in Cherry Tomatoes

DESSERTS:
   Sherbet in Orange Cups

Eggs Florentine
May be served with a choice of the following:

HORS D'OEUVRES:
Fresh Mushrooms in Double Cream
Fresh Vegetables with Tuna Dip

SOUPS:
Jellied Madrilène in Avocado Shells
Tomato Crab Bisque
Curried Lemon Soup
Chilly Crème de Menthe Soup

SALADS:
Cucumber Salad Damascus
Cauliflower Salad
Cold String Beans and Shrimp Salad

VEGETABLES:
Garlic Cherry Tomatoes
Green Onions with Lemon Clam Sauce
Carrots and White Grapes
Cauliflower with Almonds

GO WITHS:
Anchovies in Cherry Tomatoes
Grilled Cheese Tomatoes
Petite Peas in Artichoke Bottoms

DESSERTS:
Pêches Flambées
Sherbet in Orange Cups
Mousse au Chocolat

ENTREES

Breast of Chicken in Rum Crumbs
May be served with a choice of the following:

HORS D'OEUVRES:
Mushrooms Stuffed with Walnuts and Pistachios, Glazed
Fresh Figs and Walnuts in Prosciutto Ham

SOUPS:
Cream of Asparagus with Asparagus Tips and Anchovy
Croutons
Curried Lemon Soup
Cold German Fruit Soup in Cantaloupe Shells
Jellied Madrilène in Avocado Shells
Chilly Crème de Menthe Soup

SALADS:
Fruit and Cucumber Salad
Cauliflower Salad

VEGETABLES:
Fluffy Corn Fritters
Green Beans Serbian
Carrots and White Grapes
Vegetables in Cream
Green Beans and Onions au Beurre

GO WITHS:
Petite Peas in Artichoke Bottoms
Curried Pineapple

Fried Bananas
Marrons and Apricots
Glazed Apple Rings

DESSERTS:
Pêches Flambées
Apple Pancake
Crêpes Suzette
Apple Contreau Sundae
Cherry Jubilee Sundae
Cold German Fruit Soup in Cantaloupe Shells

Lobster Pernod or
Absinthe Gourmet
May be served with a choice of the following:

HORS D'OEUVRES:
Vegetables à la Grecque
Hors d'oeuvres tray, consisting of Fresh Mushrooms in
     Double Cream, Eggs à la Russe, Italian White Bean
     and Anchovy Salad, and Vegetables à la Grecque
Mushrooms Stuffed with Walnuts and Pistachios, Glazed
Ramekins of Shrimp in Sour Cream

SOUPS:
Jellied Madrilène in Avocado Shells
Tomato Crab Bisque
Cream of Asparagus Soup with Asparagus Tips and
     Anchovy Croutons

SALADS:
Cucumber Salad Damascus
Cold String Bean and Shrimp Salad
Bibb Lettuce with Green Goddess Dressing

VEGETABLES:
New Peas with Mint
Green Beans and Onions au Beurre
Grilled Cheese Tomatoes
Petite Peas in Artichoke Bottoms

DESSERTS:
Pêches Flambées
Apple Cointreau Sundae
Sherbet in Orange Cups

Boeuf Au Vin Blanc
May be served with a choice of the following:

HORS D'OEUVRES:
Vegetables à la Grecque
Fresh Mushrooms in Double Cream
Escargots in Cream
Mushrooms Stuffed with Walnuts and Pistachios, Glazed

SOUPS:
Garlic Soup with Croutons and Poached Egg
Real French Onion Soup
Cream of Asparagus Soup with Asparagus Tips and
Anchovy Croutons

SALADS:
Cucumber Salad Damascus
Onion Salad
Bibb Lettuce with Green Goddess Dressing
Caesar Salad

VEGETABLES:
Garlic Cherry Tomatoes
Green Beans Serbian
Carrots and White Grapes
New Peas with Mint
Green Beans and Onions au Beurre
Fried Green Peppers
Potato Pflutters
Baked Stuffed Cheese Potatoes

GO WITHS:
Anchovies in Cherry Tomatoes
Grilled Cheese Tomatoes

DESSERTS:
    Pêches Flambées
    Apple Cointreau Sundae
    Sherbet in Orange Cups
    Mousse au Chocolat

Calf's Liver Paris
May be served with a choice of the following:

HORS D'OEUVRES:
Vegetables à la Grecque
Mushrooms Stuffed with Walnuts and Pistachios, Glazed
Fresh Figs and Walnuts in Prosciutto Ham

SOUPS:
Garlic Soup with Croutons and Poached Egg
Jellied Madrilène in Avocado Shells
Tomato Crab Bisque
Cream of Asparagus Soup with Asparagus Tips and
    Anchovy Croutons
Chilly Crème de Menthe Soup

SALADS:
Cucumber Salad Damascus
Fruit and Cucumber Salad
Cauliflower Salad

VEGETABLES:
Carrots and White Grapes
Vegetables in Cream
Green Beans and Onions au Beurre
Fried Green Peppers
Artichokes with Foie Gras

GO WITHS:
Anchovies in Cherry Tomatoes
Petite Peas in Artichoke Bottoms
Glazed Apple Rings

DESSERTS:
Pêches Flambées
Cherries Jubilee Sundae
Apple Cointreau Sundae

Lobster-Shrimp or Crayfish in Wine Rice
May be served with a choice of the following:

HORS D'OEUVRES:
Vegetables à la Grecque
Fresh Vegetables with Tuna Dip
Fresh Mushrooms in Double Cream
Coquilles St. Jacques

SOUPS:
Jellied Madrilène in Avocado Shells
Tomato Crab Bisque
Cream of Asparagus Soup with Asparagus Tips and
Anchovy Croutons

SALADS:
Cucumber Salad Damascus
Cauliflower Salad
Bibb Lettuce with Green Goddess Dressing

VEGETABLES:
New Peas with Mint
Vegetables in Cream
Green Beans and Onions au Beurre
Fried Green Peppers

GO WITHS:
Petite Peas in Artichoke Bottoms

DESSERTS:
Pêches Flambées
Sherbet in Orange Cups
Champagne Fruit Cocktail

Bouillabaisse
May be served with a choice of the following:

HORS D'OEUVRES:
Vegetables à la Grecque
Hors d'oeuvres tray, consisting of Eggs à la Russe, Vegetables à la Grecque, Fresh Mushrooms in Double Cream, and Italian White Bean and Anchovy Salad
Mushrooms Stuffed with Walnuts and Pistachios, Glazed Escargots in Cream

SOUPS:
No soup is needed. Bouillabaisse is a soup as well as a seafood dinner

SALADS:
Cucumber Salad Damascus
Italian White Bean and Anchovy Salad
Onion Salad
Caesar Salad

VEGETABLES:
Green Beans Serbian
Green Onions with Lemon Clam Sauce
New Peas with Mint
Green Beans and Onions au Beurre

DESSERTS:
Apple Cointreau Sundae
Pêches Flambées
Sherbet in Orange Cups
Mousse au Chocolat

Shrimp Curry
May be served with a choice of the following:

HORS D'OEUVRES:
Mushrooms Stuffed with Walnuts and Pistachios, Glazed
Fresh Figs and Walnuts in Prosciutto Ham

SOUPS:
Garlic Soup with Croutons and Poached Egg
Jellied Madrilène in Avocado Shells
Tomato Crab Bisque
Chilly Crème de Menthe Soup

SALADS:
Cucumber Salad Damascus
Onion Salad
Lebanese Salad
Fruit and Cucumber Salad
Cauliflower Salad

VEGETABLES:
Garlic Cherry Tomatoes
Green Beans Serbian
Green Onions with Lemon Clam Sauce
Carrots with White Grapes
New Peas with Mint
Cauliflower with Almonds
Vegetables in Cream
Green Beans and Onions au Beurre
Fried Green Peppers

GO WITHS:
Curried Pineapple
Fried Bananas

Flaming Spiced Peaches
Marrons and Apricots

DESSERTS:
Pêches Flambées
Strawberry Trifle
Sherbet in Orange Cups
Apple Cointreau Sundae

Kidneys Flambé
May be served with a choice of the following:

HORS D'OEUVRES:

Mushrooms Stuffed with Walnuts and Pistachios, Glazed
Fresh Figs and Walnuts in Prosciutto Ham

SOUPS:

Garlic Soup with Croutons and Poached Egg
Jellied Madrilène in Avocado Shells
Real French Onion Soup
Chilly Crème de Menthe Soup

SALADS:

Cucumber Salad Damascus
Cauliflower Salad
Onion Salad
Bibb Lettuce with Green Goddess
Caesar Salad

VEGETABLES:

Vegetables in Cream
Green Beans and Onions au Beurre
Fried Green Peppers
Garlic Cherry Tomatoes
Green Beans Serbian
Carrots and White Grapes
New Peas with Mint
Cauliflower with Almonds
Potato Pflutters
Baked Stuffed Cheese Potatoes

GO WITHS:

Glazed Apple Rings
Grilled Cheese Tomatoes
Petite Peas in Artichoke Bottoms

DESSERTS:

Apple Pancake
Apple Cointreau Sundae
Cherry Jubilee Sundae
Mousse au Chocolat
Sherbet in Orange Cups
Cold German Fruit Soup in Cantaloupe Shells

Spaghetti with White Clam Sauce
May be served with a choice of the following:

HORS D'OEUVRES:
  Italian Antipasto
  Vegetables à la Grecque
  Fresh Figs and Walnuts in Prosciutto Ham
  Mozzarella in Carrozza

SOUPS:
  Garlic Soup with Croutons and Poached Egg

SALADS:
  Italian White Bean and Anchovy Salad
  Onion Salad
  Cauliflower Salad
  Cold String Bean and Shrimp Salad

VEGETABLES:
  Garlic Cherry Tomatoes
  Green Beans Serbian
  Green Beans and Onions au Beurre
  Fried Green Peppers

GO WITHS:
  Anchovies in Cherry Tomatoes, except when using
      Anchovy Salad

DESSERTS:
  Sherbet in Orange Cups

Breast of Chicken Perigourdine
May be served with a choice of the following:

HORS D'OEUVRES:
 Vegetables à la Grecque
 Fresh Mushrooms in Double Cream
 Mushrooms Stuffed with Walnuts and Pistachios, Glazed
 Fresh Figs and Walnuts in Prosciutto Ham
 Coquilles St. Jacques

SOUPS:
 Jellied Madrilène in Avocado Shells
 Tomato Crab Bisque
 Real French Onion Soup
 Cream of Asparagus with Asparagus Tips and Anchovy
  Croutons

SALADS:
 Cucumber Salad Damascus
 Fruit and Cucumber Salad
 Cold String Beans and Shrimp Salad

VEGETABLES:
 Green Beans Serbian
 Green Onions with Lemon Clam Sauce
 Carrots and White Grapes
 New Peas and Onions au Beurre
 Potato Pflutters

DESSERTS:
 Crêpes Suzette
 Pêches Flambées
 Mousse au Chocolat
 Sherbet in Orange Cups

Escargots Bourguignonne
May be served with a choice of the following:

HORS D'OEUVRES:
Vegetable à la Grecque
Fresh Mushrooms in Double Cream
Mushrooms Stuffed with Walnuts and Pistachios, Glazed
Coquilles St. Jacques

SOUPS:
Jellied Madrilène in Avocado Shells
Real French Onion Soup

SALADS:
Cucumber Salad Damascus
Cauliflower Salad
Bibb Lettuce with Green Goddess Dressing
Caesar Salad

VEGETABLES:
Green Beans Serbian
New Peas with Mint
Vegetables in Cream
Green Beans and Onions au Beurre

DESSERTS:
Crêpes Suzette
Pêches Flambées
Apple Cointreau Sundae
Sherbet in Orange Cups
Mousse au Chocolat

Shrimp Flambé
May be served with a choice of the following:

HORS D'OEUVRES:
Mushrooms Stuffed with Walnuts and Pistachios, Glazed
Fresh Figs and Walnuts in Prosciutto Ham
Coquilles St. Jacques

SOUPS:
Jellied Madrilène in Avocado Shells
Real French Onion Soup
Cream of Asparagus Soup with Asparagus Tips and
Anchovy Croutons

SALADS:
Cucumber Salad Damascus
Cauliflower Salad
Fruit and Cucumber Salad

VEGETABLES:
Green Beans Serbian
Green Onions with Lemon Clam Sauce
New Peas with Mint
Vegetables in Cream
Green Beans and Onions au Beurre
Artichokes with Foie Gras
Grilled Cheese Tomatoes
Petite Peas in Artichoke Bottoms

DESSERTS:
Pêches Flambées
Sherbet in Orange Cups
Mousse au Chocolat

Shrimp Scampi
May be served with a choice of the following:

HORS D'OEUVRES:
   Italian Antipasto
   Vegetables à la Grecque
   Mozzarella in Carrozza

SOUPS:
   Jellied Madrilène in Avocado Shells
   Tomato Crab Bisque
   Gazpacho
   Curried Lemon Soup
   Chilly Crème de Menthe Soup

SALADS:
   Italian White Bean and Anchovy Salad
   Cucumber Salad Damascus
   Onion Salad
   Cauliflower Salad
   Lebanese Salad
   Caesar Salad

VEGETABLES:
   Green Beans Serbian
   Green Onions with Lemon Clam Sauce
   New Peas with Mint
   Green Beans and Onions au Beurre
   Fried Green Peppers
   Grilled Cheese Tomatoes
   Potato Pflutters

GO WITHS:
   Anchovies in Cherry Tomatoes

DESSERTS:
   Pêches Flambées
   Greek Pontica
   Sherbet in Orange Cups

Danish Fish with Blue Cheese
May be served with a choice of the following:

HORS D'OEUVRES:
Vegetables à la Grecque
Eggs à la Russe

SOUPS:
Jellied Madrilène in Avocado Shells
Garlic Soup with Croutons and Poached Egg
Cream of Asparagus with Asparagus Tips and Anchovy
Croutons
Curried Lemon Soup

SALADS:
Onion Salad
Cucumber Salad Damascus
Cold String Bean and Shrimp Salad

VEGETABLES:
Vegetables in Cream
Green Beans and Onions au Beurre
Fried Green Peppers
Green Beans Serbian
New Peas with Mint
Potato Pflutters

DESSERTS:
Pêches Flambées
Apple Cointreau Sundae

COOKING OUT GOURMET STYLE

Chicken Livers and White Grapes
May be served with a choice of the following:

HORS D'OEUVRES:
   Fresh Mushrooms in Double Cream
   Mushrooms Stuffed with Walnuts and Pistachios, Glazed
   Fresh Figs and Walnuts in Prosciutto Ham

SALADS:
   Cucumber Salad Damascus
   Fruit and Cucumber Salad

VEGETABLES:
   Green Beans Serbian
   New Peas with Mint
   Cauliflower with Almonds

GO WITHS:
   Glazed Apple Rings
   Flaming Spiced Peaches
   Marrons and Apricots
   Petite Peas in Artichoke Bottoms
   Curried Pineapple Slices

DESSERTS:
   Champagne Fruit Cocktail
   Pêches Flambées
   Apple Pancake

Apple Cointreau Sundae
Cherries Jubilee Sundae
Fruit en Brochette
Sherbet in Orange Cups
Cold German Fruit Soup

Scallops and Cherry Tomatoes
May be served with a choice of the following:

HORS D'OEUVRES:
   Italian Antipasto
   Vegetables à la Grecque
   Fresh Vegetables in Tuna Dip
   Pineapple, Shrimp, Chicken Livers, and Olives en Brochette

SALADS:
   Italian White Bean and Anchovy Salad
   Onion Salad
   Cauliflower Salad
   Lebanese Salad
   Caesar Salad
   Asparagus and Smoked Salmon Salad
   Coquilles St. Jacques Salad

VEGETABLES:
   Green Beans Serbian
   Baked Cheese Potatoes
   Green Onions with Lemon Clam Sauce
   New Peas with Mint
   Fried Green Peppers

DESSERTS:
   Fruit en Brochette
   Sherbet in Orange Cups
   Cherries Jubilee Sundae

Steak Kebobs
May be served with a choice of the following:

HORS D'OEUVRES:
Italian Antipasto
Vegetables à la Grecque
Pineapple, Shrimp, Chicken Livers, and Olives en Brochette

SALADS:
Cucumber Salad Damascus
Onion Salad
Lebanese Salad
Cauliflower Salad
Italian White Bean and Anchovy Salad
Caesar Salad

VEGETABLES:
Garlic Cherry Tomatoes
Green Beans Serbian
Baked Stuffed Cheese Potatoes

DESSERTS:
Fruit en Brochette
Apple Cointreau Sundae
Cherries Jubilee Sundae
Sherbet in Orange Cups

Ginger-Shrimp Kebobs
May be served with a choice of the following:

HORS D'OEUVRES:
Italian Antipasto
Eggs à la Russe
Fresh Vegetables with Tuna Dip

SALADS:
Cucumber Salad Damascus
Lebanese Salad
Cauliflower Salad
Caesar Salad

VEGETABLES:
Garlic Cherry Tomatoes
Green Beans Serbian
Green Beans and Onions au Beurre
Fried Green Peppers

DESSERTS:
Pêches Flambées
Fruit en Brochette
Sherbet in Orange Cups

Chicken, Pineapple, and
Sweet Potato Kebobs
   May be served with a choice of the following:

HORS D'OEUVRES:
   Eggs à la Russe
   Fresh Figs and Walnuts in Prosciutto Ham
   Mushrooms Stuffed with Walnuts and Pistachios, Glazed

SALADS:
   Cucumber Salad Damascus
   Fruit and Cucumber Salad
   Cauliflower Salad

VEGETABLES:
   Fluffy Corn Fritters
   Green Beans Serbian
   Carrots and White Grapes

GO WITHS:
   Flaming Spiced Peaches
   Fried Bananas

DESSERTS:
   Apple Cointreau Sundae
   Cherries Jubilee Sundae
   Fruit en Brochette
   Sherbet in Orange Cups

MIDNIGHT SNACKS

Creamed Crabmeat and Oysters
   May be served with a choice of the following:

SALADS:
   Cucumber Salad Damascus
   Fruit and Cucumber Salad
   Cauliflower Salad
   Caesar Salad
   Cold String Bean and Shrimp Salad

VEGETABLES:
   Garlic Cherry Tomatoes
   Green Onions with Lemon Clam Sauce
   Carrots and White Grapes
   New Peas with Mint
   Vegetables in Cream
   Green Beans and Onions au Beurre
   Artichokes with Foie Gras

GO WITHS:
   Anchovies in Cherry Tomatoes
   Petite Peas in Artichoke Bottoms

DESSERTS:
   Crêpes Suzette
   Pêches Flambées
   Apple Cointreau Sundae
   Sherbet in Orange Cups
   Mousse au Chocolat

Lobster à la Newburg
May be served with a choice of the following:

SALADS:
    Cucumber Salad Damascus
    Cauliflower Salad
    Caesar Salad
    Cold String Bean and Shrimp Salad

VEGETABLES:
    Green Onions with Lemon Clam Sauce
    Carrots and White Grapes
    New Peas with Mint
    Vegetables in Cream
    Green Beans and Onions au Beurre
    Artichokes with Foie Gras

GO WITHS:
    Grilled Cheese Tomatoes
    Petite Peas in Artichoke Bottoms

DESSERTS:
    Sherbet in Orange Cups
    Champagne Fruit Cocktail
    Crêpes Suzette
    Pêches Flambées
    Apple Cointreau Sundae
    Cherries Jubilee Sundae

Swiss Fondue
May be served with a choice of the following:

DESSERTS:
Champagne Fruit Cocktail
Pêches Flambées

Lobster Stew
May be served with a choice of the following:

SALADS:
Caesar Salad
Cold String Bean and Shrimp Salad

DESSERTS:
Sherbet in Orange Cups

Sukiyaki
May be served with a choice of the following:

SALADS:

Cucumber Salad Damascus
Cold String Bean and Shrimp Salad

DESSERTS:

Sherbet in Orange Cups
Fruit en Brochette
Apple Cointreau Sundae

Welsh Rarebit
May be served with a choice of the following:

SALADS:
Cucumber Salad Damascus
Caesar Salad
Cold String Bean and Shrimp Salad

VEGETABLES:
Green Beans Serbian
New Peas with Mint

GO WITHS:
Grilled Cheese Tomatoes
Petite Peas in Artichoke Bottoms

DESSERTS:
Pêches Flambées
Sherbet in Orange Cups
Mousse au Chocolat

BE VERSATILE

Frequently dishes can be used interchangeably. For example, Ramekins of Shrimp in Sour Cream, which is often served as an hors d'oeuvre, nimbly turns into a midnight snack when served at the witching hour. Following are others that are equally versatile.

May be served as a main course for

MIDNIGHT SNACKS
Shrimp Curry
Spaghetti with White Clam
  Sauce
Caesar Salad
Campagne Fruit Cocktail
Tartar Sandwiches
Escargots in Cream
Eggs Florentine
Ramekins of Shrimp in Sour
  Cream
Shrimps Flambé
Shrimp Scampi
Escargots Bourguignonne
Boeuf au Vin Blanc

LUNCHES
Fruit and Cucumber Salad
Shrimp Curry
Caesar Salad
Tartar Sandwiches
Escargots in Cream
Potato Clam Chowder
Ramekins of Shrimp in Sour
  Cream
Lobster Stew
Danish Fish with Blue Cheese
Shrimps Flambé
Shrimp Scampi
Coquilles St. Jacques

Index